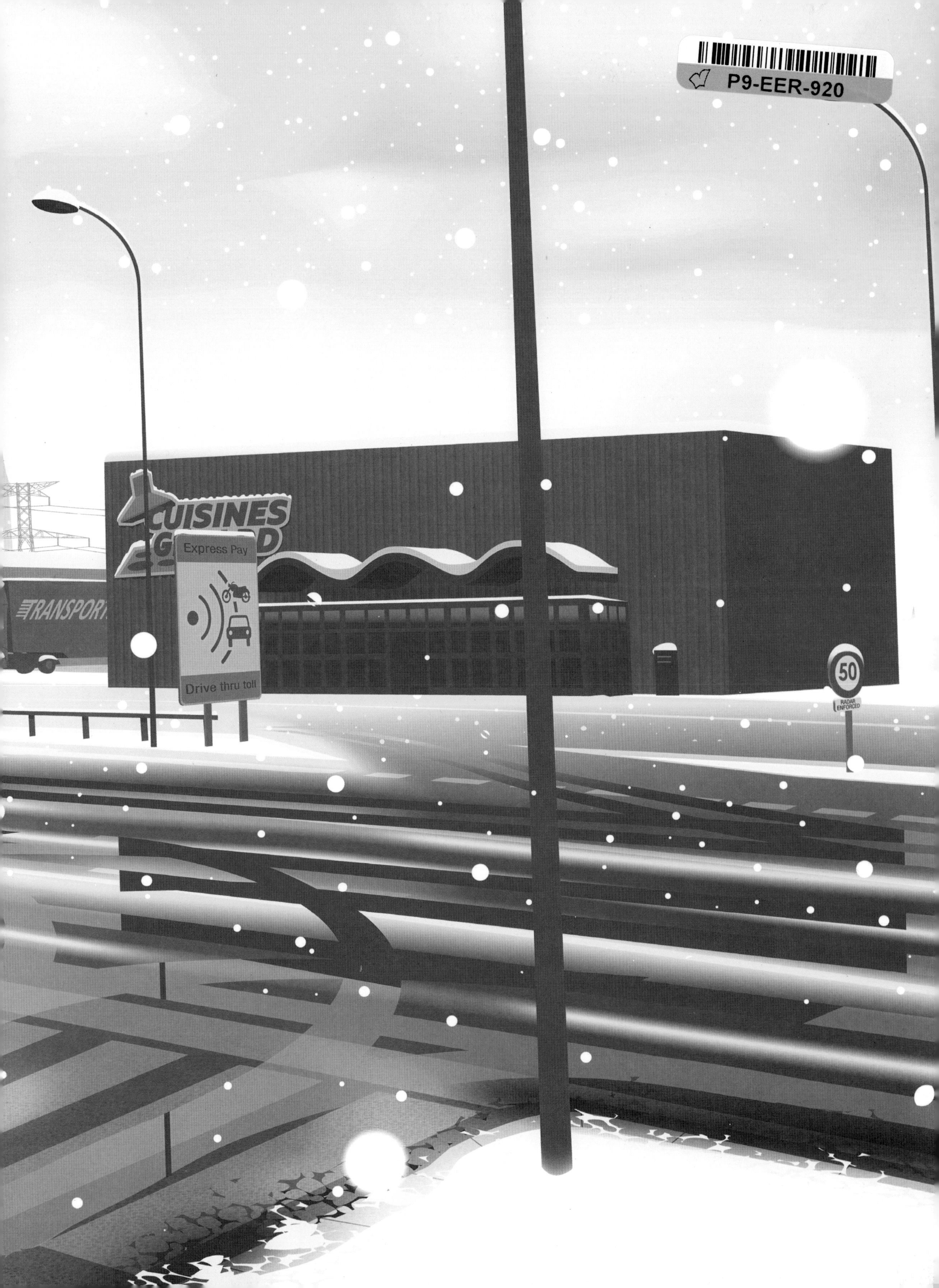
CUISINES
Express Pay
Drive thru toll
TRANSPORT
50
RADAR ENFORCED

ARTHUR DE PINS

Zombillenium

4. Royal Witchcraft

Zombillenium presents
NIGHT ON BALD MOUNTAIN
INSPIRED BY THE SYMPHONY BY
MUSSORGSKY

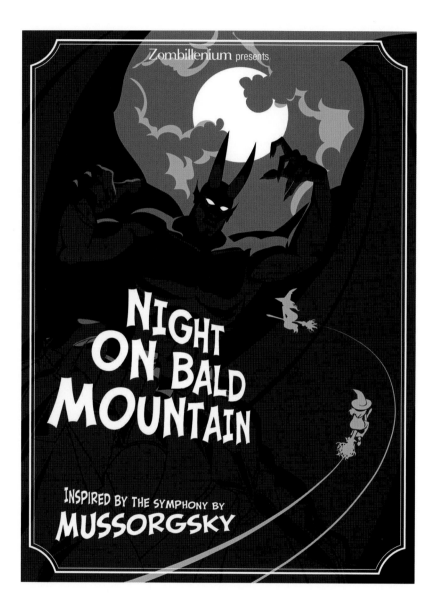

nbm GRAPHIC NOVELS
Nantier • Beall • Minoustchine
NEW YORK

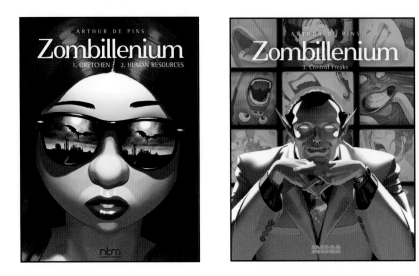

Also available:
Zombillenium, vols.1 & 2 combo
Vol.3

SEE MORE AND ORDER AT NBMPUB.COM

ALSO AVAILABLE WHEREVER EBOOKS ARE SOLD.

We have over 200 titles available
NBM
160 Broadway, Suite 700, East Wing
New York, NY 10038
Catalog available by request

Thanks to Caroline for her support.
Thanks to Mel and Fred for their invaluable advice on police matters and to the brasserie
Archimalt in Chambery for letting me visit the brewery.
Finally, thank you to TeamZombie for 5 fabulous years spent bringing this to the big
screen.
All that team energy has imbued this volume as well.
(Which was, as always, created on Illustrator 9.0 but this time, cover included.)

ARTHUR DE PINS

ISBN 9781681122199
© DUPUIS 2018, by De Pins
www.dupuis.com
Originally published in French as "Zombillénium 4. La Fille de l'air"
All rights reserved.
© 2019 NBM for the English translation
Translation by Joe Johnson
Lettering by Ortho

Printed in India
First printing July 2019

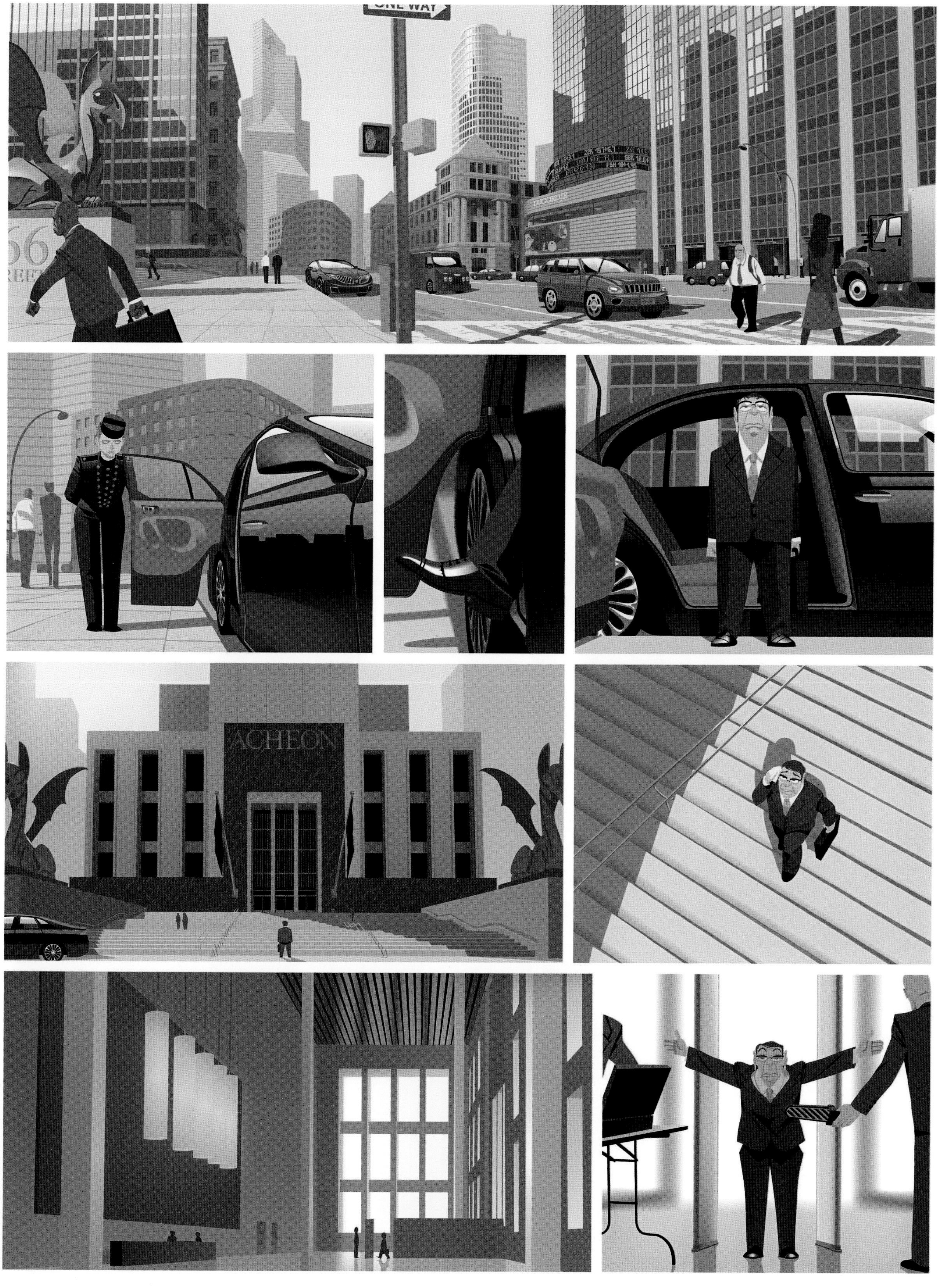
ONE WAY
ACHEON

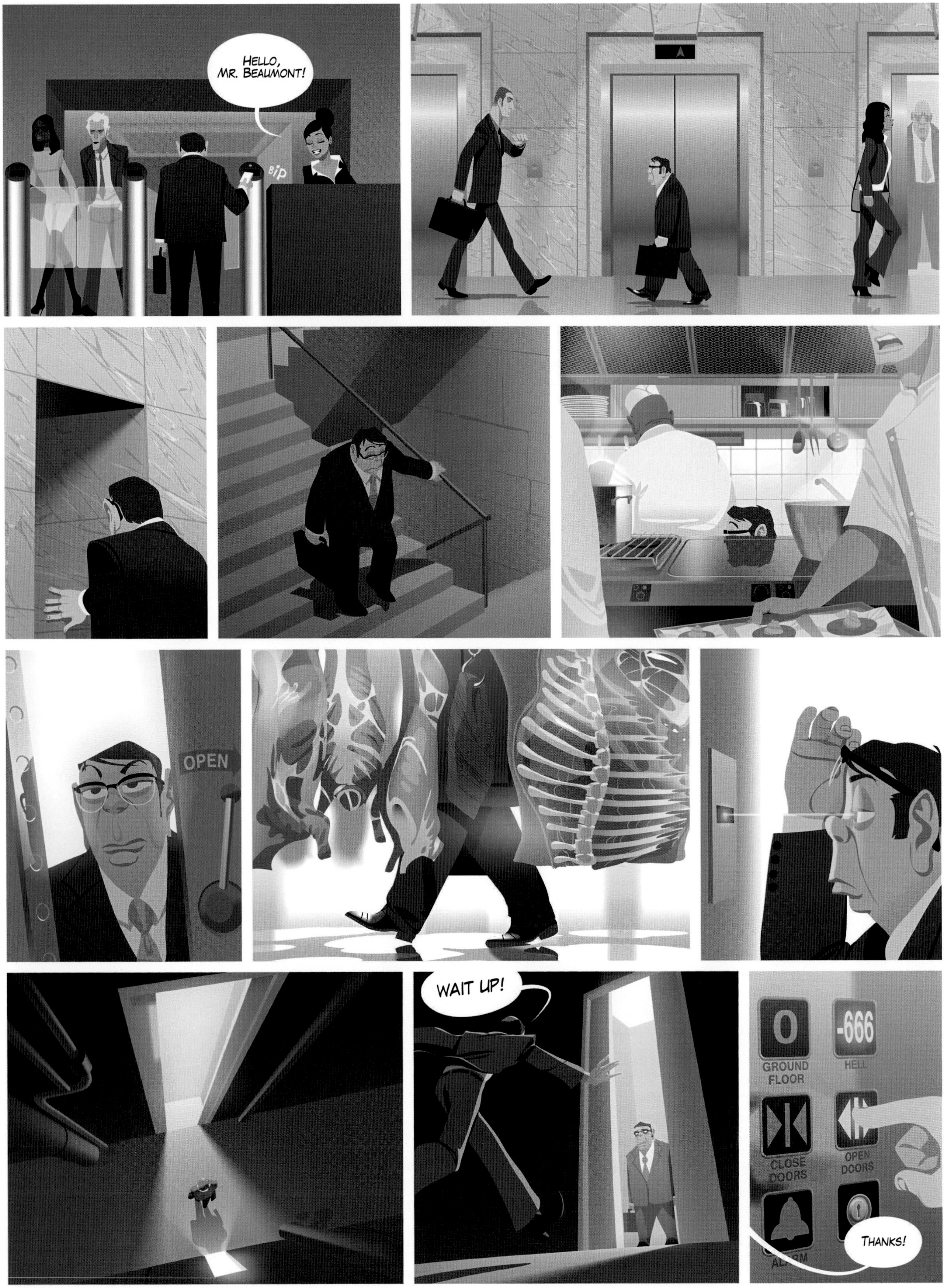
HELLO, MR. BEAUMONT!
BIP
OPEN
WAIT UP!
0
GROUND FLOOR
-666
HELL
CLOSE DOORS
OPEN DOORS
ALARM
THANKS!

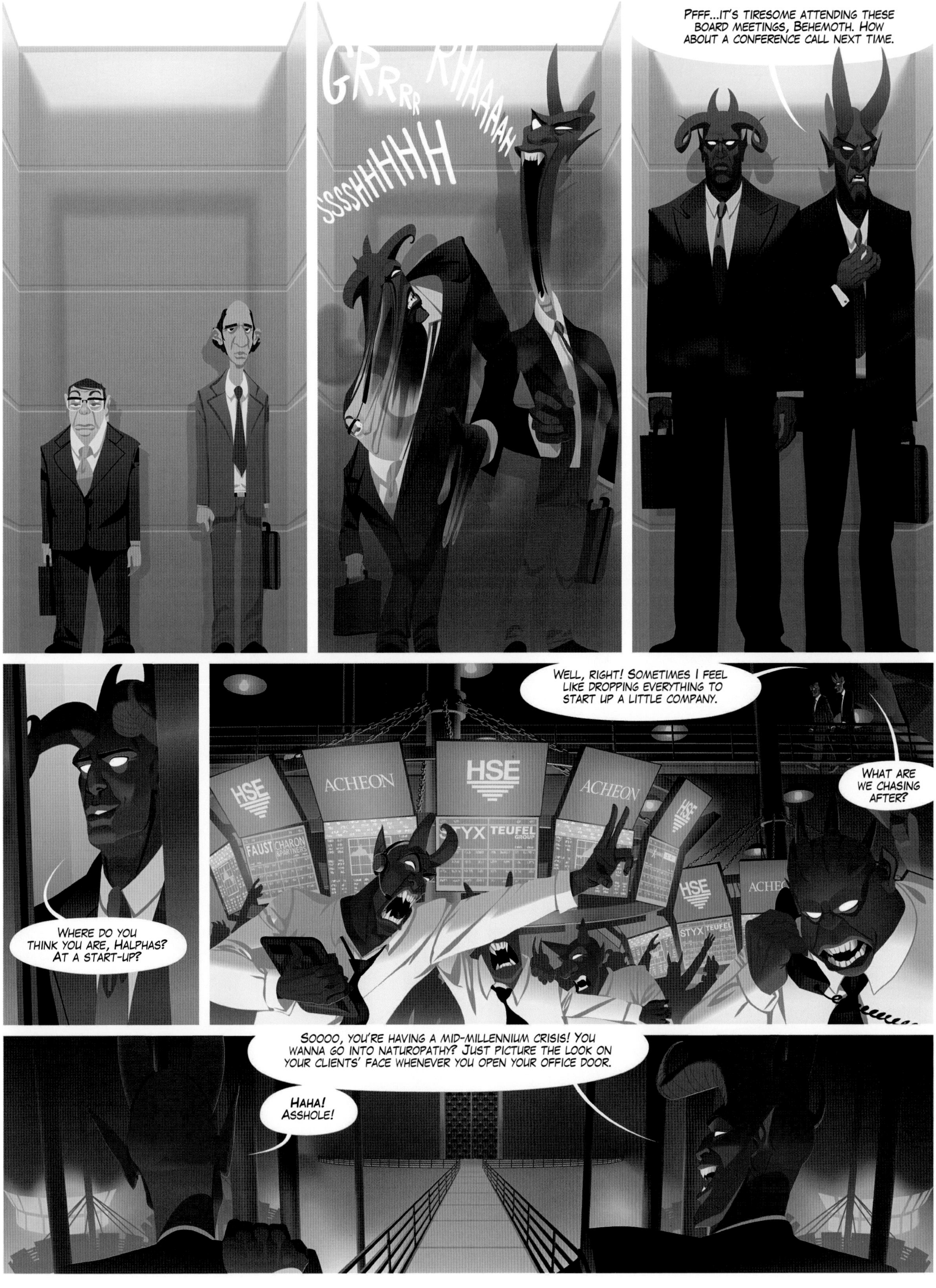
GRRRRR
SSSSHHHHH
RHAAAAAH
PFFF...IT'S TIRESOME ATTENDING THESE BOARD MEETINGS, BEHEMOTH. HOW ABOUT A CONFERENCE CALL NEXT TIME.
WHERE DO YOU THINK YOU ARE, HALPHAS? AT A START-UP?
WELL, RIGHT! SOMETIMES I FEEL LIKE DROPPING EVERYTHING TO START UP A LITTLE COMPANY.
WHAT ARE WE CHASING AFTER?
HSE
ACHEON
FAUST
CHARON & PARTNERS
STYX
TEUFEL GROUP
SOOOO, YOU'RE HAVING A MID-MILLENNIUM CRISIS! YOU WANNA GO INTO NATUROPATHY? JUST PICTURE THE LOOK ON YOUR CLIENTS' FACE WHENEVER YOU OPEN YOUR OFFICE DOOR.
HAHA! ASSHOLE!

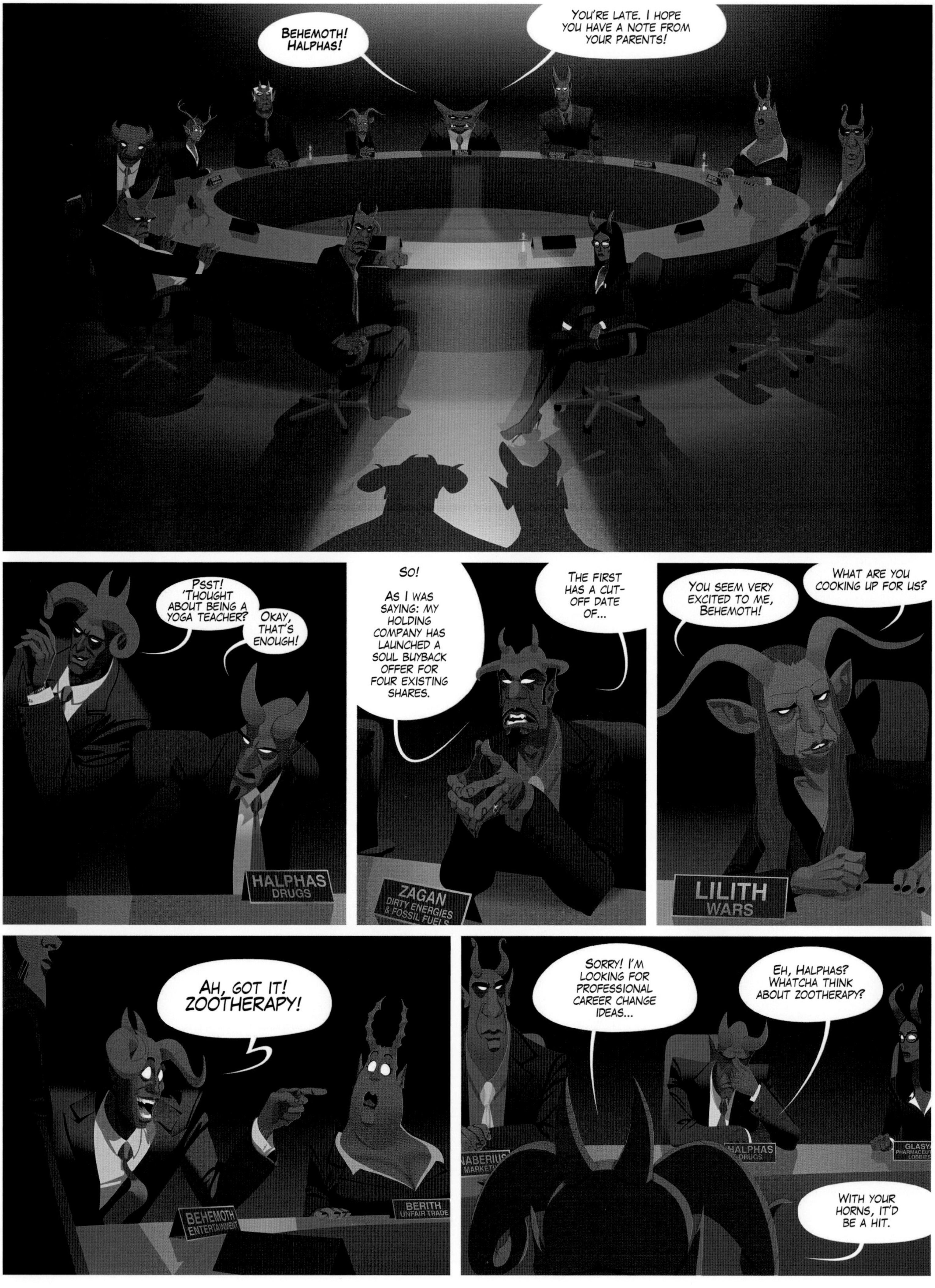
BEHEMOTH! HALPHAS!
YOU'RE LATE. I HOPE YOU HAVE A NOTE FROM YOUR PARENTS!
PSST! 'THOUGHT ABOUT BEING A YOGA TEACHER?
OKAY, THAT'S ENOUGH!
HALPHAS
DRUGS
SO!
AS I WAS SAYING: MY HOLDING COMPANY HAS LAUNCHED A SOUL BUYBACK OFFER FOR FOUR EXISTING SHARES.
THE FIRST HAS A CUT-OFF DATE OF...
ZAGAN
DIRTY ENERGIES & FOSSIL FUELS
YOU SEEM VERY EXCITED TO ME, BEHEMOTH!
WHAT ARE YOU COOKING UP FOR US?
LILITH
WARS
AH, GOT IT! ZOOTHERAPY!
BEHEMOTH
ENTERTAINMENT
BERITH
UNFAIR TRADE
SORRY! I'M LOOKING FOR PROFESSIONAL CAREER CHANGE IDEAS...
EH, HALPHAS? WHATCHA THINK ABOUT ZOOTHERAPY?
HALPHAS
DRUGS
WITH YOUR HORNS, IT'D BE A HIT.

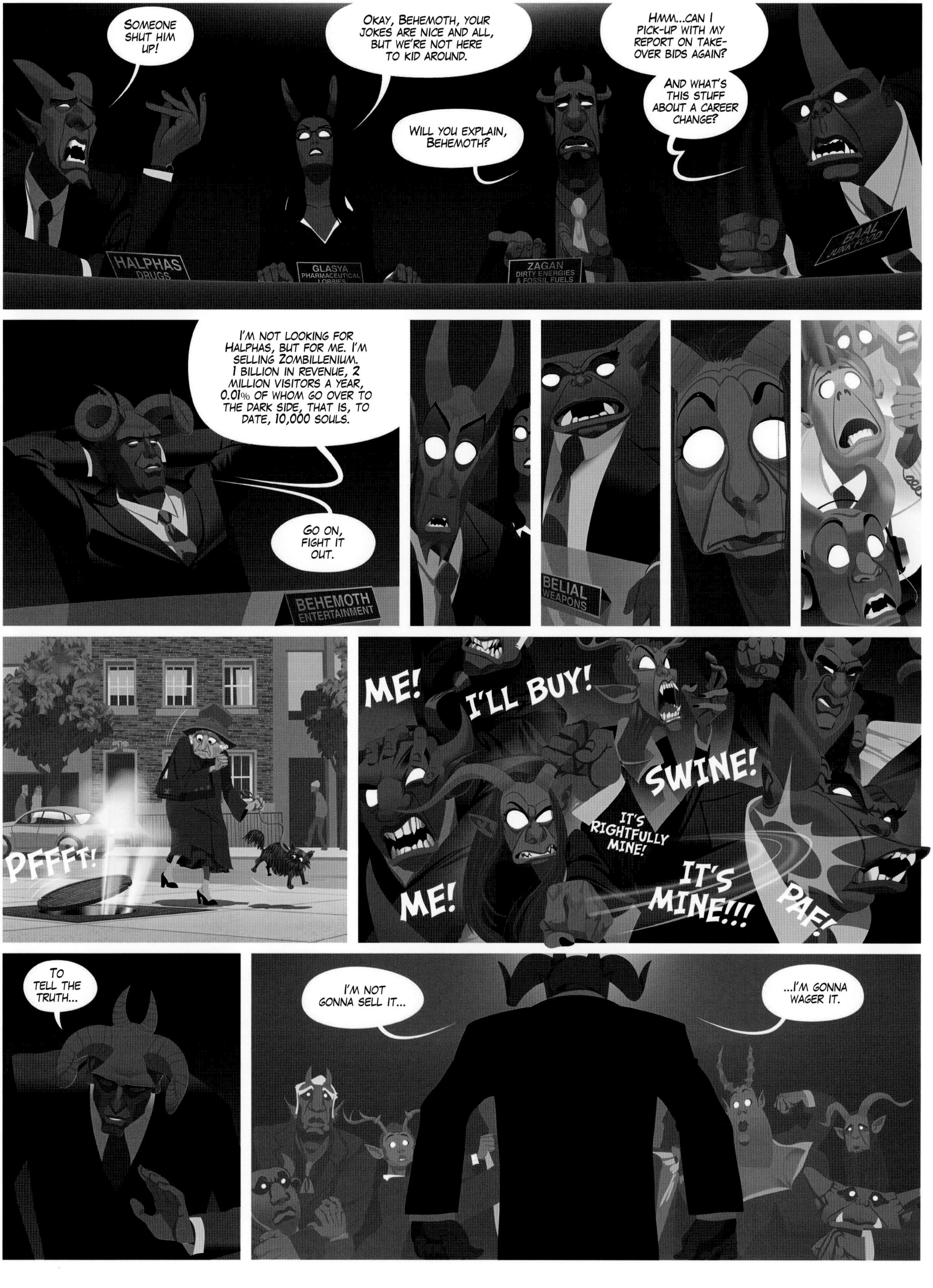

Someone shut him up!
Okay, Behemoth, your jokes are nice and all, but we're not here to kid around.
Will you explain, Behemoth?
Hmm...can I pick-up with my report on take-over bids again?
And what's this stuff about a career change?
HALPHAS DRUGS
GLASYA PHARMACEUTICAL LOBBIES
ZAGAN DIRTY ENERGIES & FOSSIL FUELS
BAAL JUNK FOOD
I'm not looking for Halphas, but for me. I'm selling Zombillenium. 1 billion in revenue, 2 million visitors a year, 0.01% of whom go over to the dark side, that is, to date, 10,000 souls.
Go on, fight it out.
BEHEMOTH ENTERTAINMENT
BELIAL WEAPONS
PFFFT!
ME!
I'LL BUY!
SWINE!
IT'S RIGHTFULLY MINE!
ME!
IT'S MINE!!!
PAF!
To tell the truth...
I'm not gonna sell it...
...I'm gonna wager it.

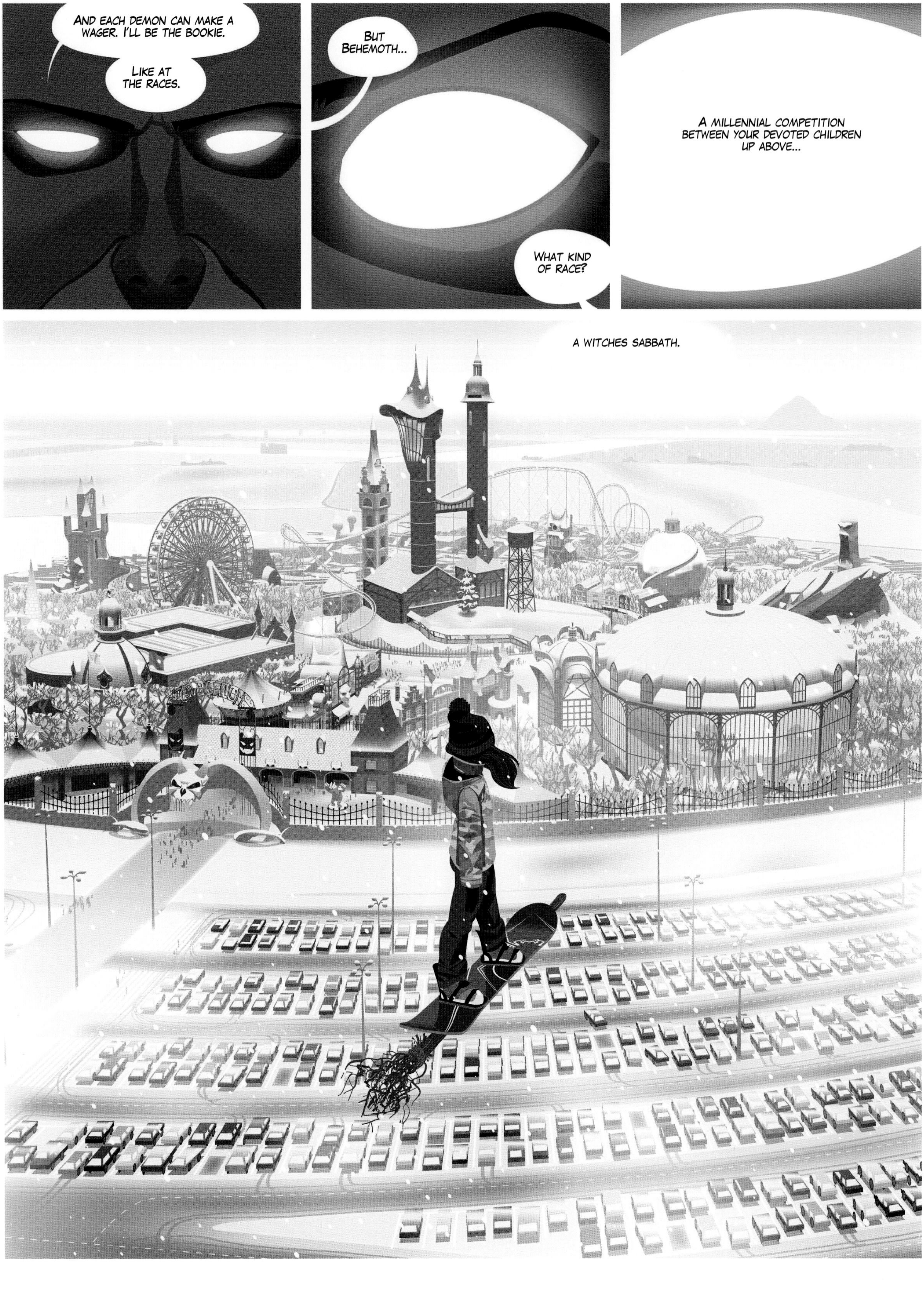
And each demon can make a wager. I'll be the bookie.
Like at the races.
But Behemoth...
What kind of race?
A millennial competition between your devoted children up above...
A witches sabbath.

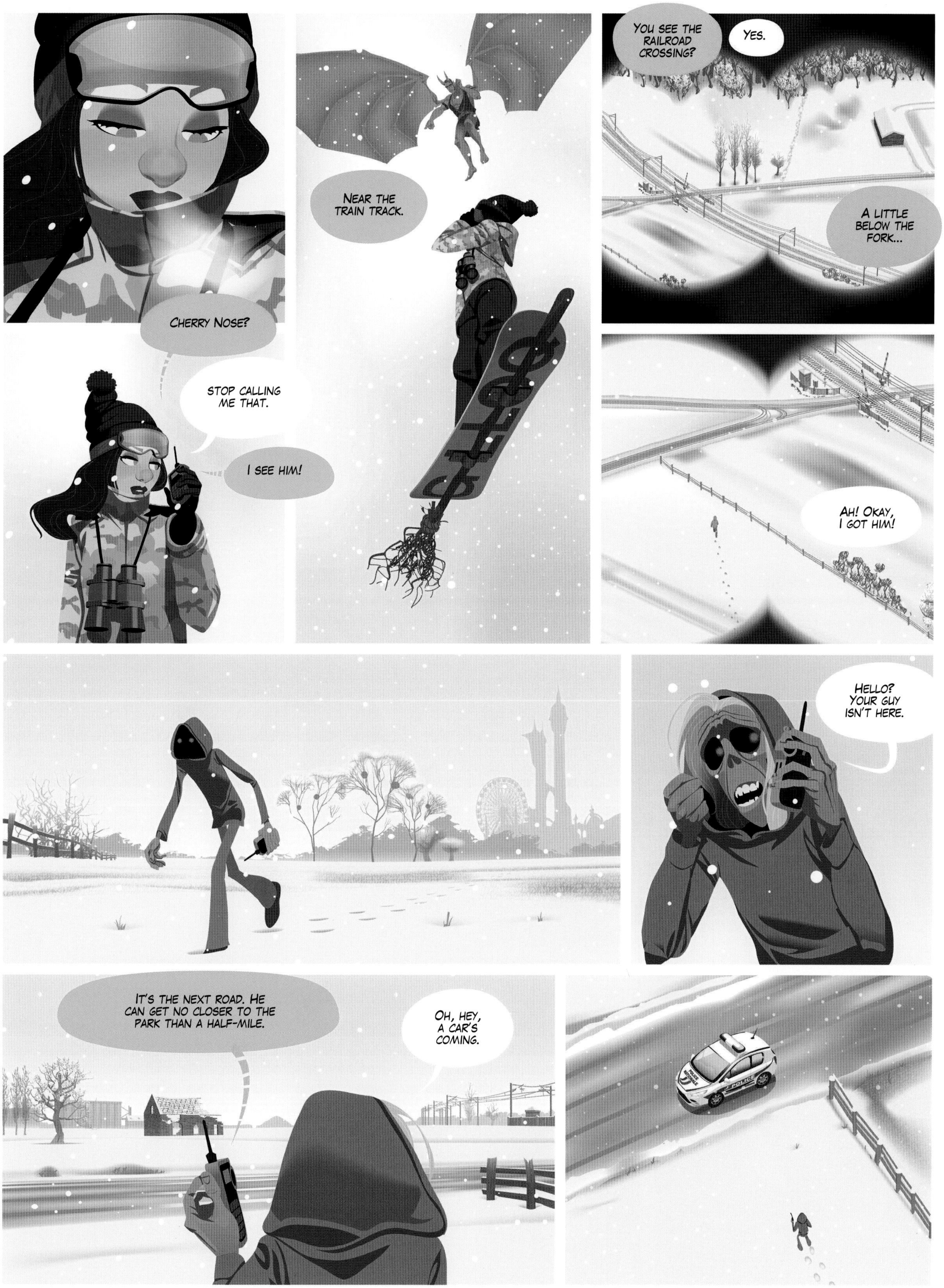
Cherry Nose?
Near the train track.
You see the railroad crossing?
Yes.
A little below the fork...
Stop calling me that.
I see him!
Ah! Okay, I got him!
Hello? Your guy isn't here.
It's the next road. He can get no closer to the park than a half-mile.
Oh, hey, a car's coming.
POLICE

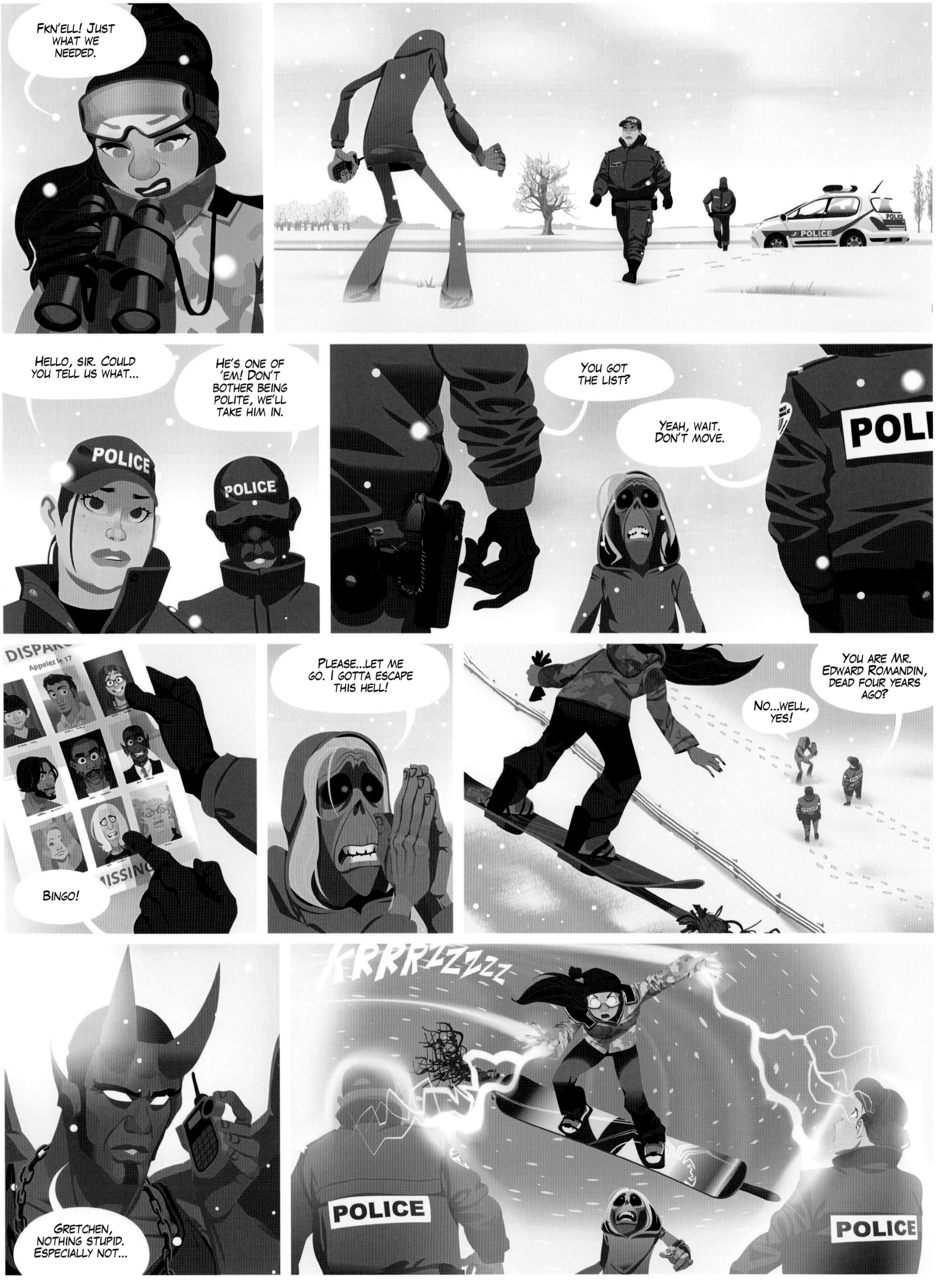
FKN'ELL! JUST WHAT WE NEEDED.
POLICE
POLICE
HELLO, SIR. COULD YOU TELL US WHAT...
HE'S ONE OF 'EM! DON'T BOTHER BEING POLITE, WE'LL TAKE HIM IN.
POLICE
POLICE
YOU GOT THE LIST?
YEAH, WAIT. DON'T MOVE.
POLI
DISPAR
Appelez le 17
MISSING
BINGO!
PLEASE...LET ME GO. I GOTTA ESCAPE THIS HELL!
YOU ARE MR. EDWARD ROMANDIN, DEAD FOUR YEARS AGO?
NO...WELL, YES!
GRETCHEN, NOTHING STUPID. ESPECIALLY NOT...
KRRRZZZZZ
POLICE
POLICE

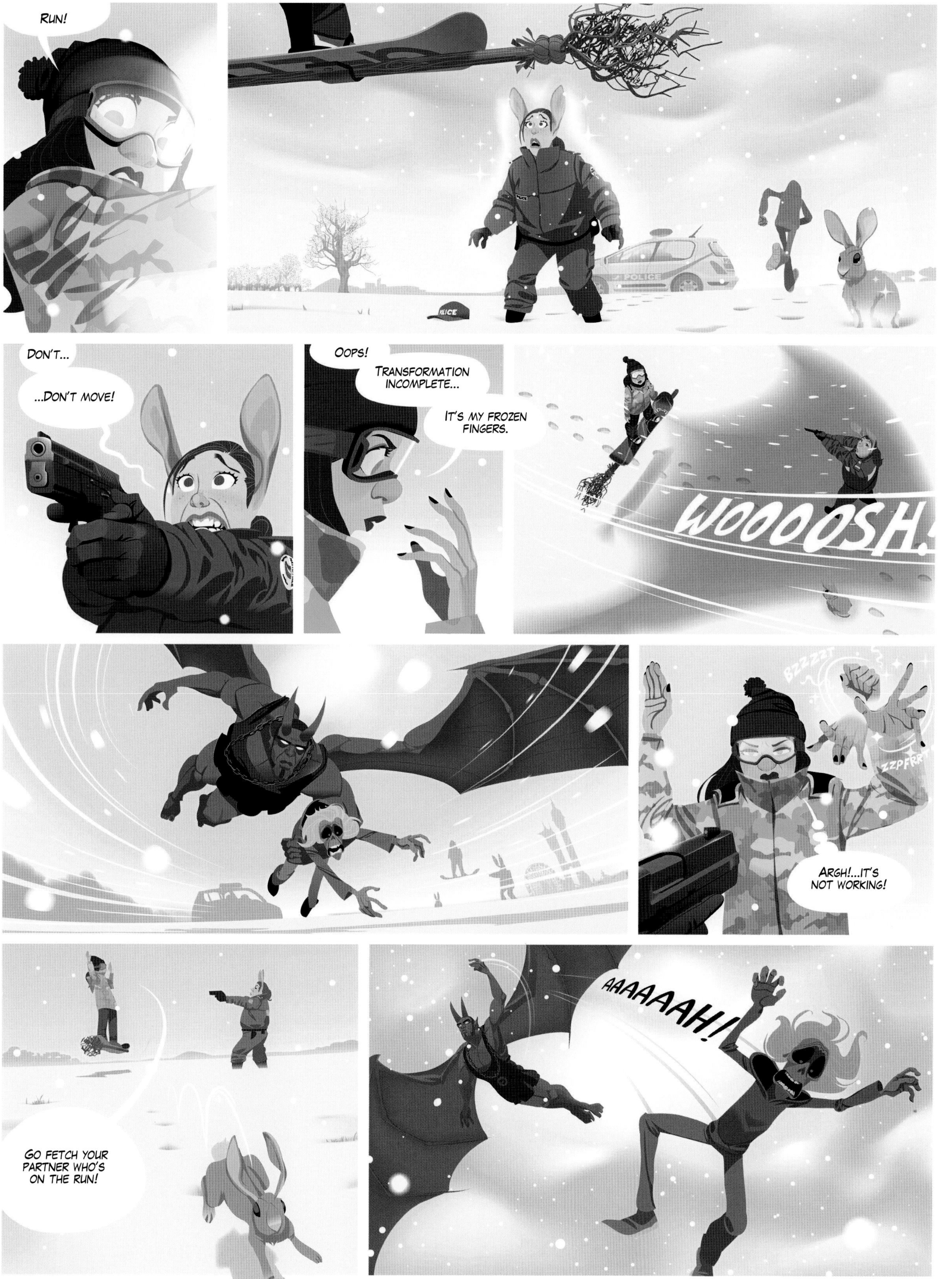

Run!
Don't...
...Don't move!
Oops!
Transformation incomplete...
It's my frozen fingers.
WOOOOSH.
BZZZZT
ZZPFRR
Argh!...it's not working!
Go fetch your partner who's on the run!
AAAAAAH!

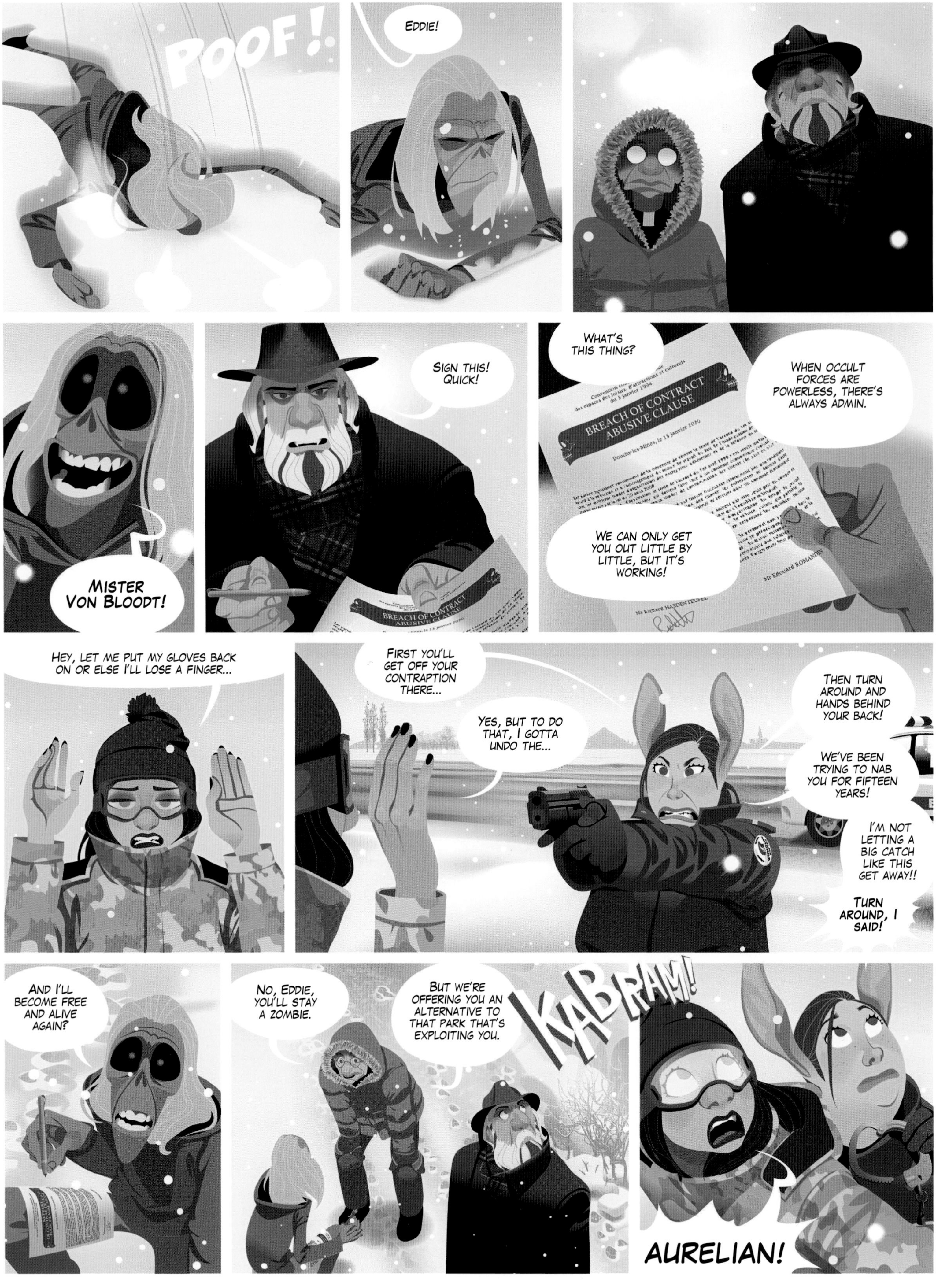
POOF!
EDDIE!
MISTER VON BLOODT!
SIGN THIS! QUICK!
BREACH OF CONTRACT
ABUSIVE CLAUSE
WHAT'S THIS THING?
WHEN OCCULT FORCES ARE POWERLESS, THERE'S ALWAYS ADMIN.
BREACH OF CONTRACT
ABUSIVE CLAUSE
WE CAN ONLY GET YOU OUT LITTLE BY LITTLE, BUT IT'S WORKING!
HEY, LET ME PUT MY GLOVES BACK ON OR ELSE I'LL LOSE A FINGER...
FIRST YOU'LL GET OFF YOUR CONTRAPTION THERE...
YES, BUT TO DO THAT, I GOTTA UNDO THE...
THEN TURN AROUND AND HANDS BEHIND YOUR BACK!
WE'VE BEEN TRYING TO NAB YOU FOR FIFTEEN YEARS!
I'M NOT LETTING A BIG CATCH LIKE THIS GET AWAY!!
TURN AROUND, I SAID!
AND I'LL BECOME FREE AND ALIVE AGAIN?
NO, EDDIE, YOU'LL STAY A ZOMBIE.
BUT WE'RE OFFERING YOU AN ALTERNATIVE TO THAT PARK THAT'S EXPLOITING YOU.
KABRAM!
AURELIAN!

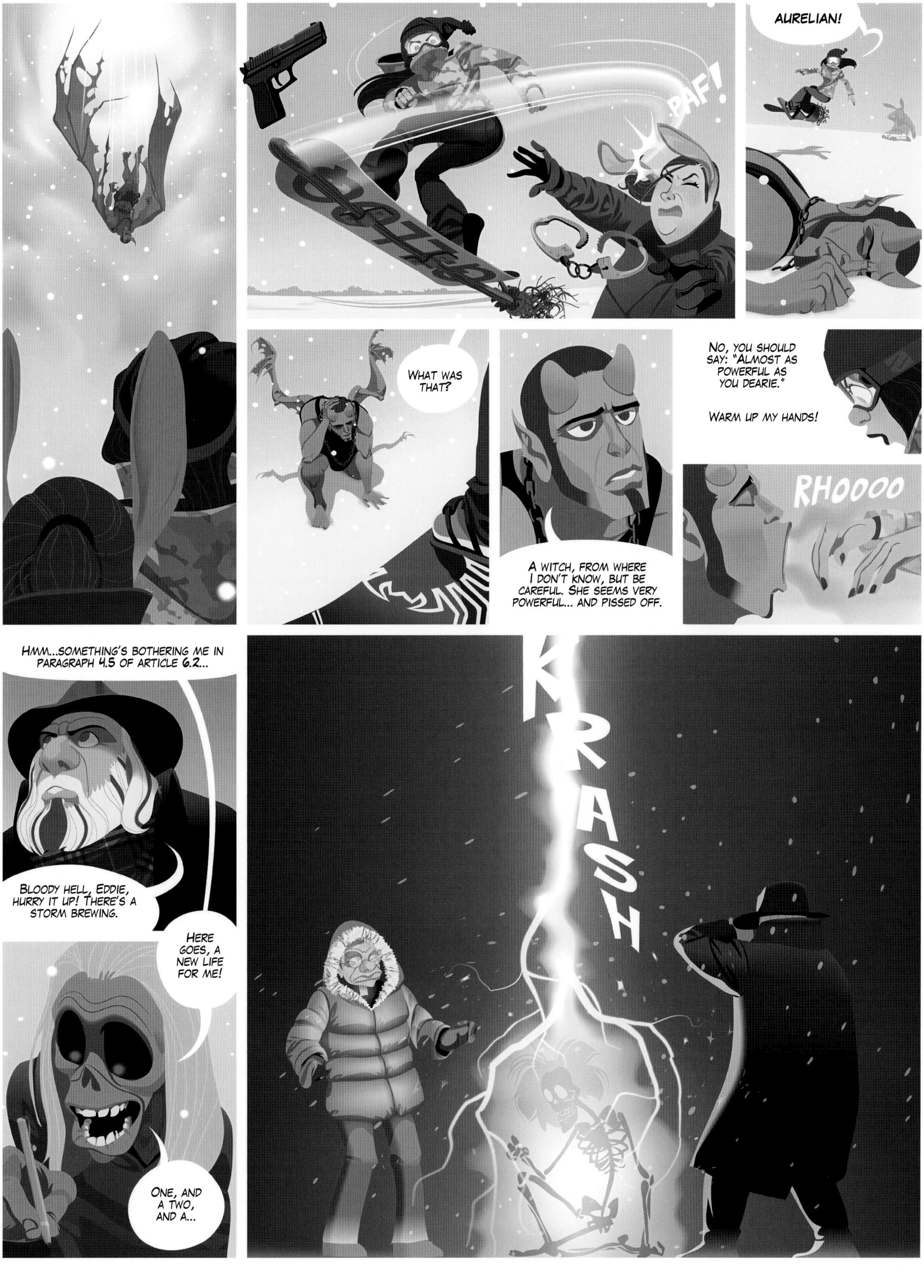
PAF!
AURELIAN!
WHAT WAS THAT?
A WITCH, FROM WHERE I DON'T KNOW, BUT BE CAREFUL. SHE SEEMS VERY POWERFUL... AND PISSED OFF.
NO, YOU SHOULD SAY: "ALMOST AS POWERFUL AS YOU DEARIE."
WARM UP MY HANDS!
RHOOOO
HMM...SOMETHING'S BOTHERING ME IN PARAGRAPH 4.5 OF ARTICLE 6.2...
BLOODY HELL, EDDIE, HURRY IT UP! THERE'S A STORM BREWING.
HERE GOES, A NEW LIFE FOR ME!
ONE, AND A TWO, AND A...
KRASH

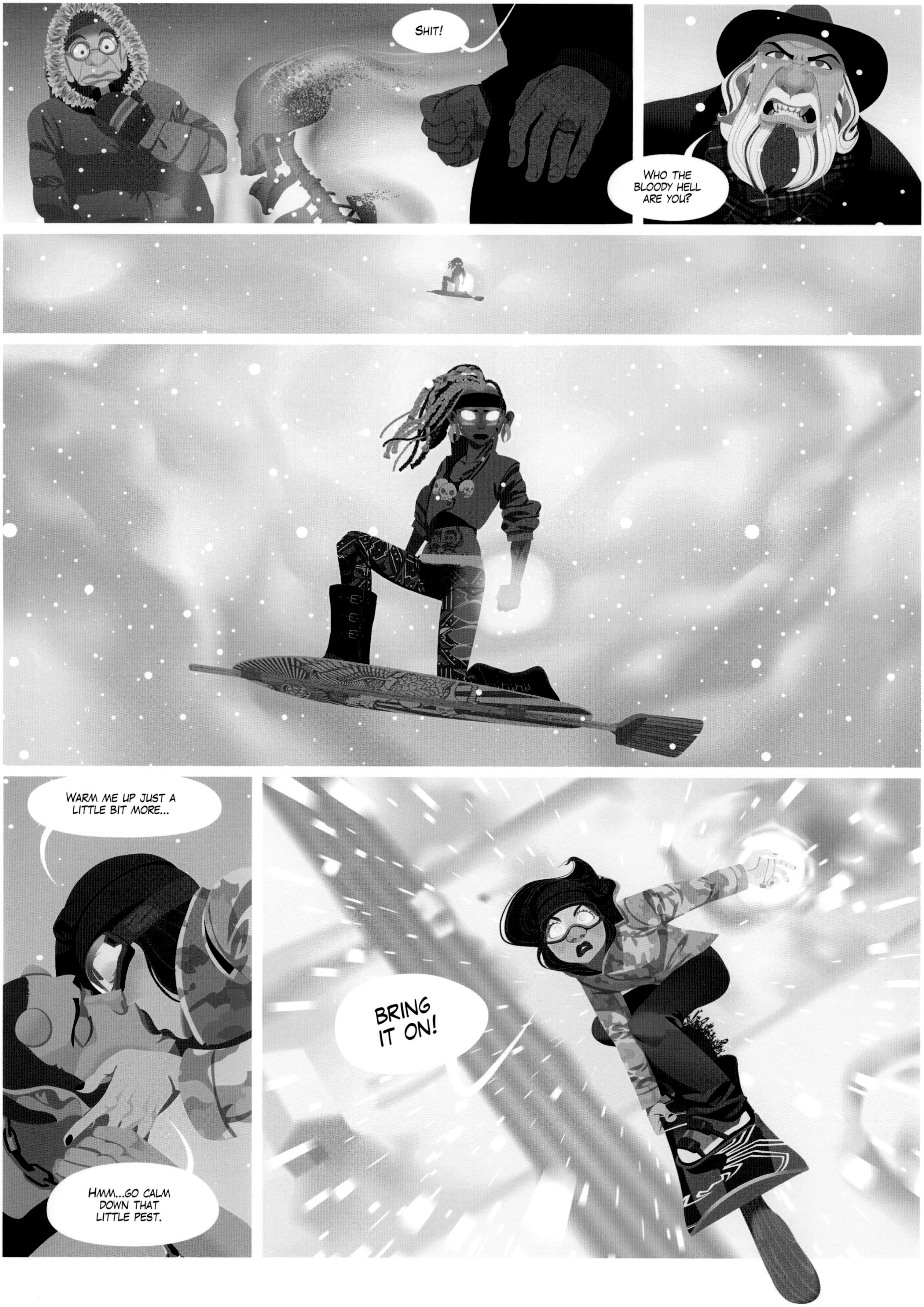
SHIT!
WHO THE BLOODY HELL ARE YOU?
WARM ME UP JUST A LITTLE BIT MORE...
HMM...GO CALM DOWN THAT LITTLE PEST.
BRING IT ON!

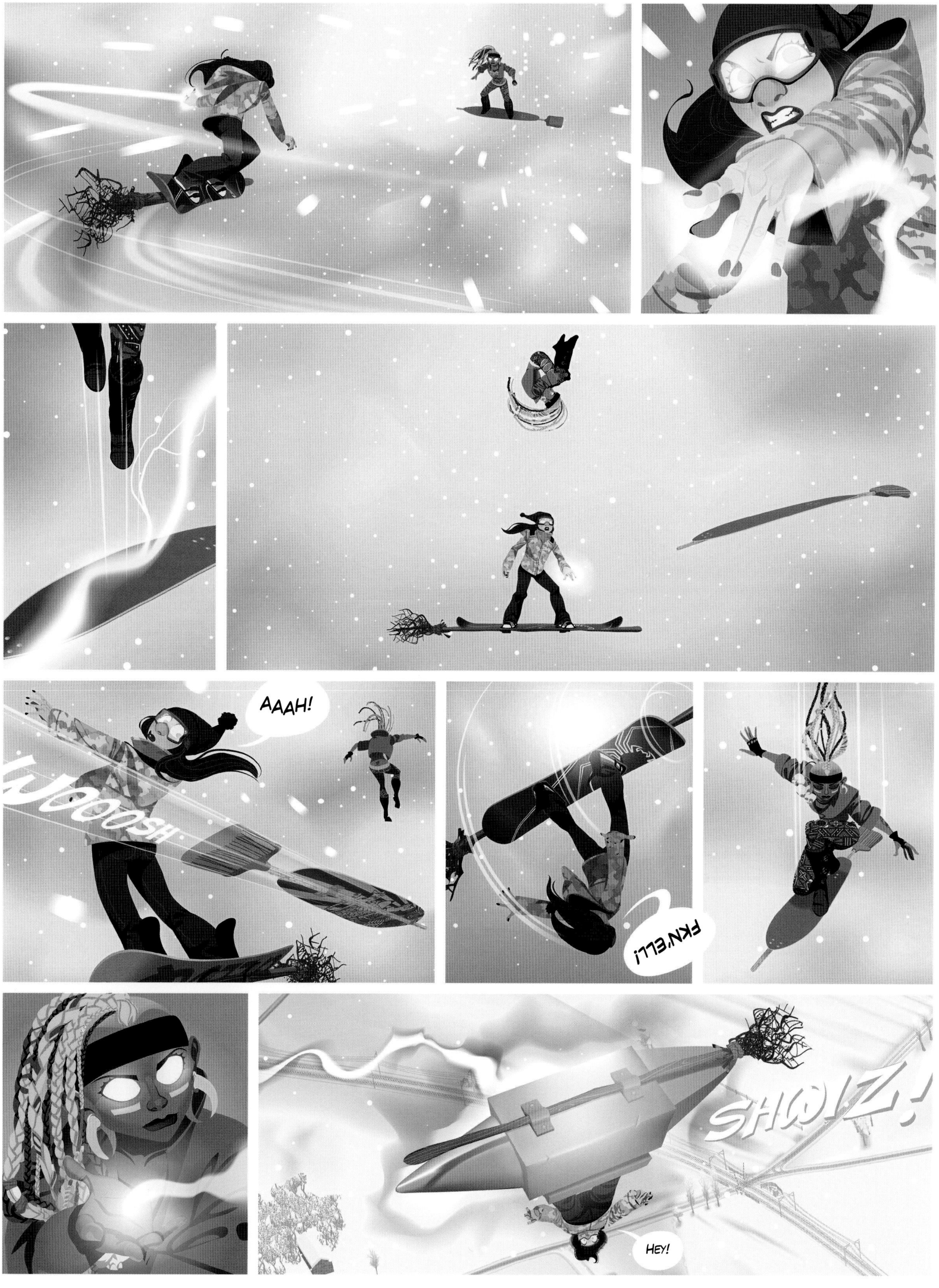
AAAH!
WOOOSH
FKN'ELL!
SHWIZ!
HEY!

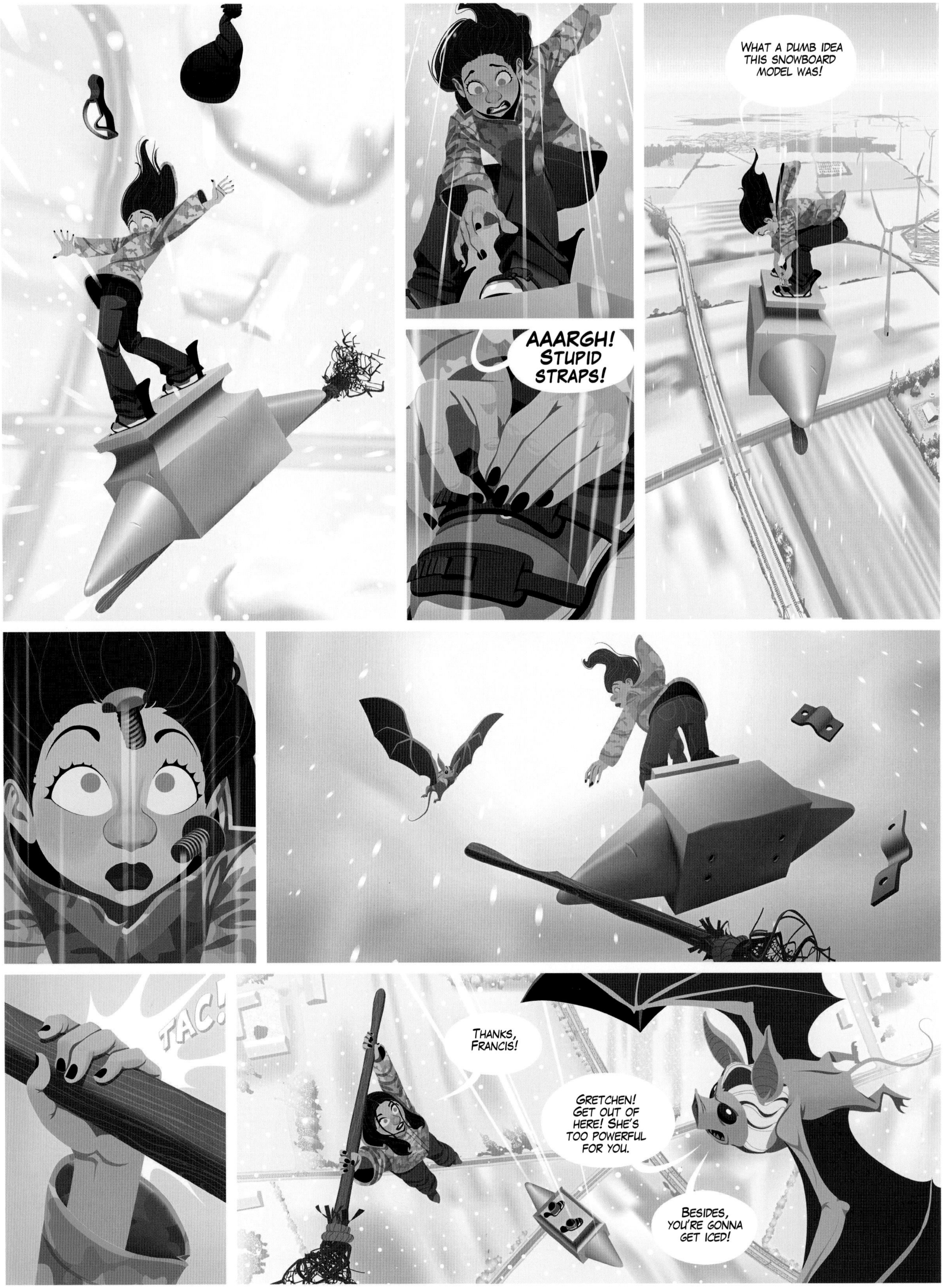
WHAT A DUMB IDEA THIS SNOWBOARD MODEL WAS!
AAARGH! STUPID STRAPS!
TAC!
THANKS, FRANCIS!
GRETCHEN! GET OUT OF HERE! SHE'S TOO POWERFUL FOR YOU.
BESIDES, YOU'RE GONNA GET ICED!

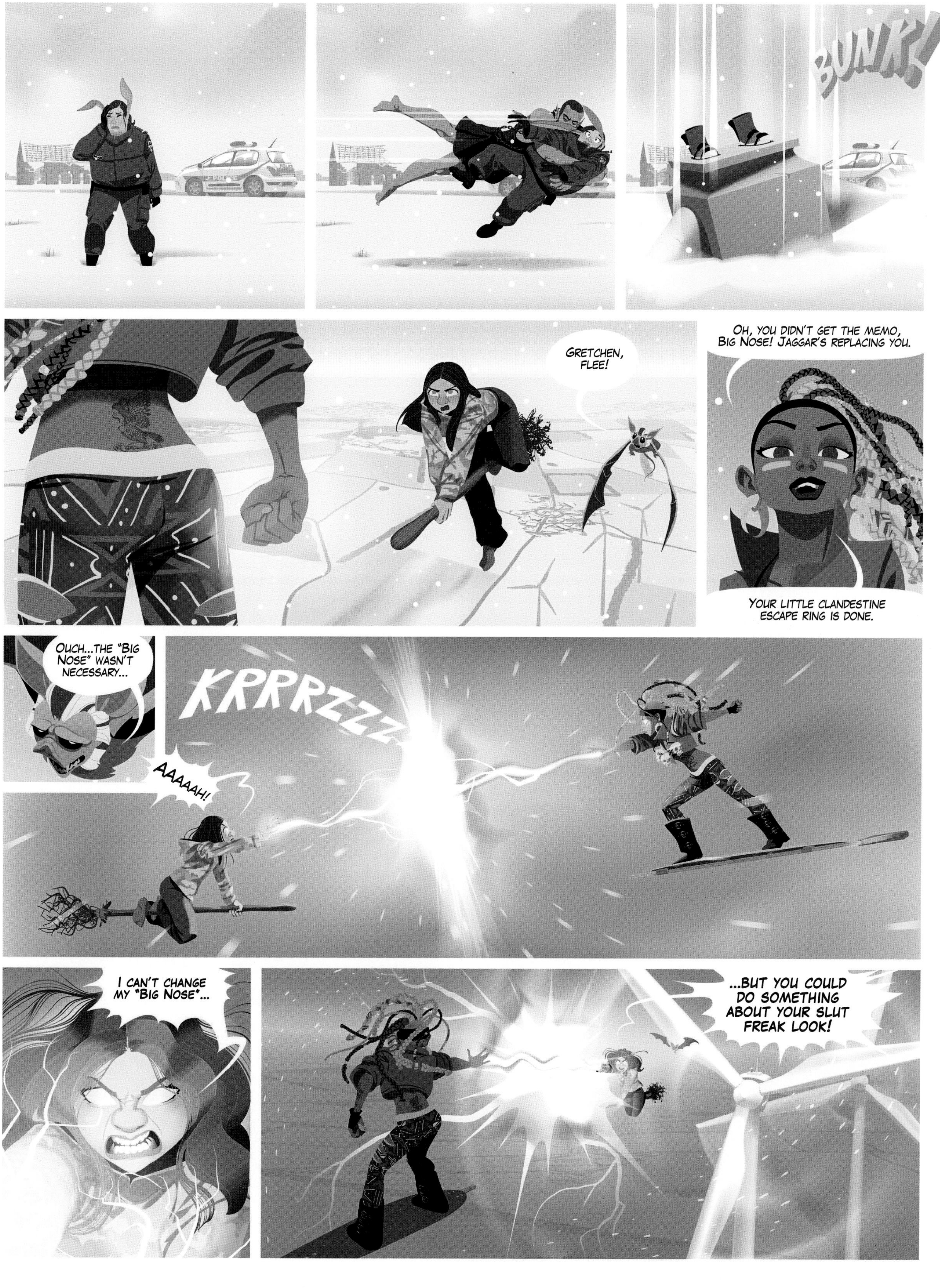
BUNK!
GRETCHEN, FLEE!
OH, YOU DIDN'T GET THE MEMO, BIG NOSE! JAGGAR'S REPLACING YOU.
YOUR LITTLE CLANDESTINE ESCAPE RING IS DONE.
OUCH...THE "BIG NOSE" WASN'T NECESSARY...
KRRRZZZZ
AAAAAH!
I CAN'T CHANGE MY "BIG NOSE"...
...BUT YOU COULD DO SOMETHING ABOUT YOUR SLUT FREAK LOOK!

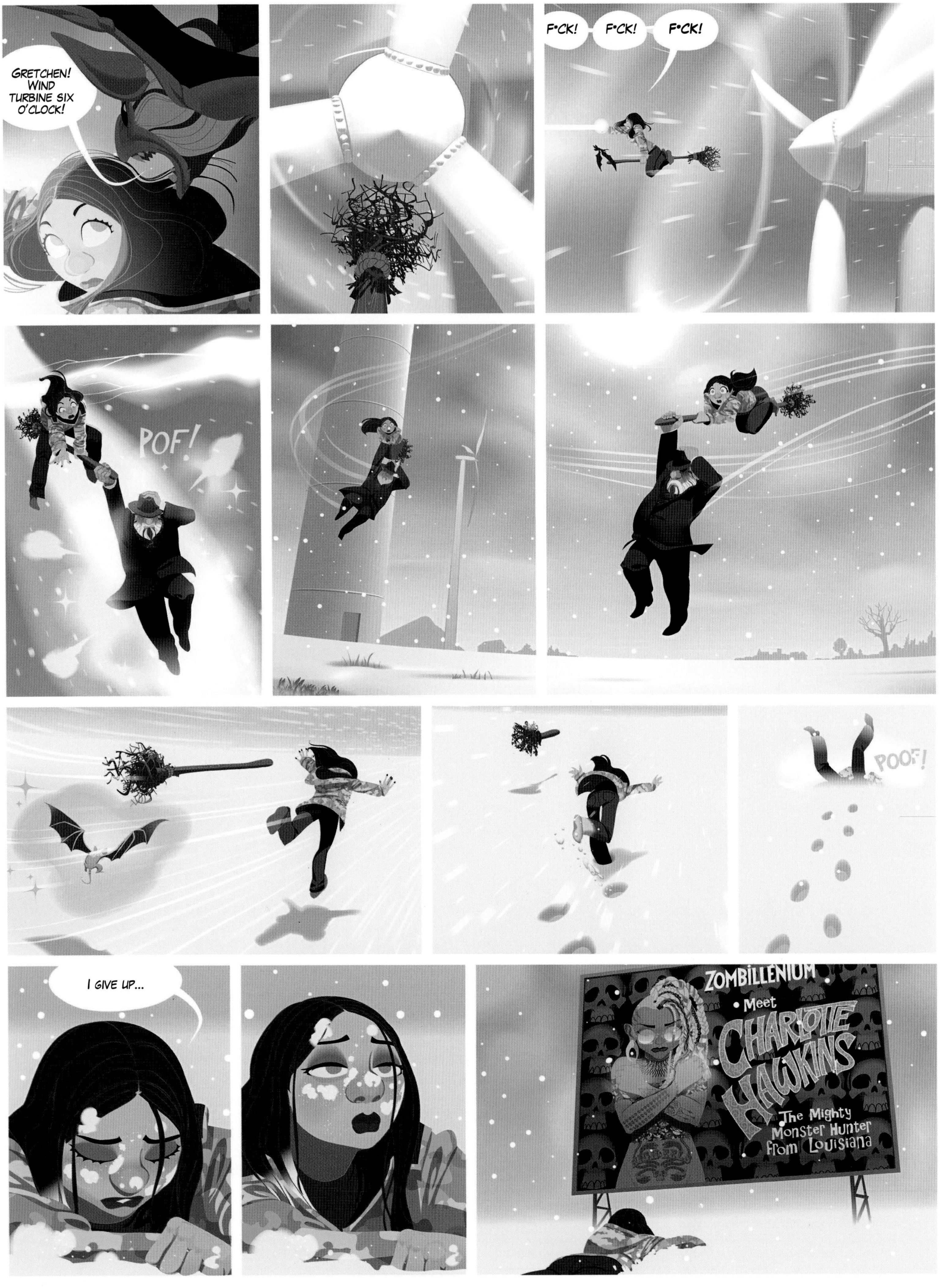
GRETCHEN! WIND TURBINE SIX O'CLOCK!
F*CK! F*CK! F*CK!
POF!
POOF!
I GIVE UP...
ZOMBILLENIUM
Meet
CHARLOTTE HAWKINS
The Mighty Monster Hunter from Louisiana

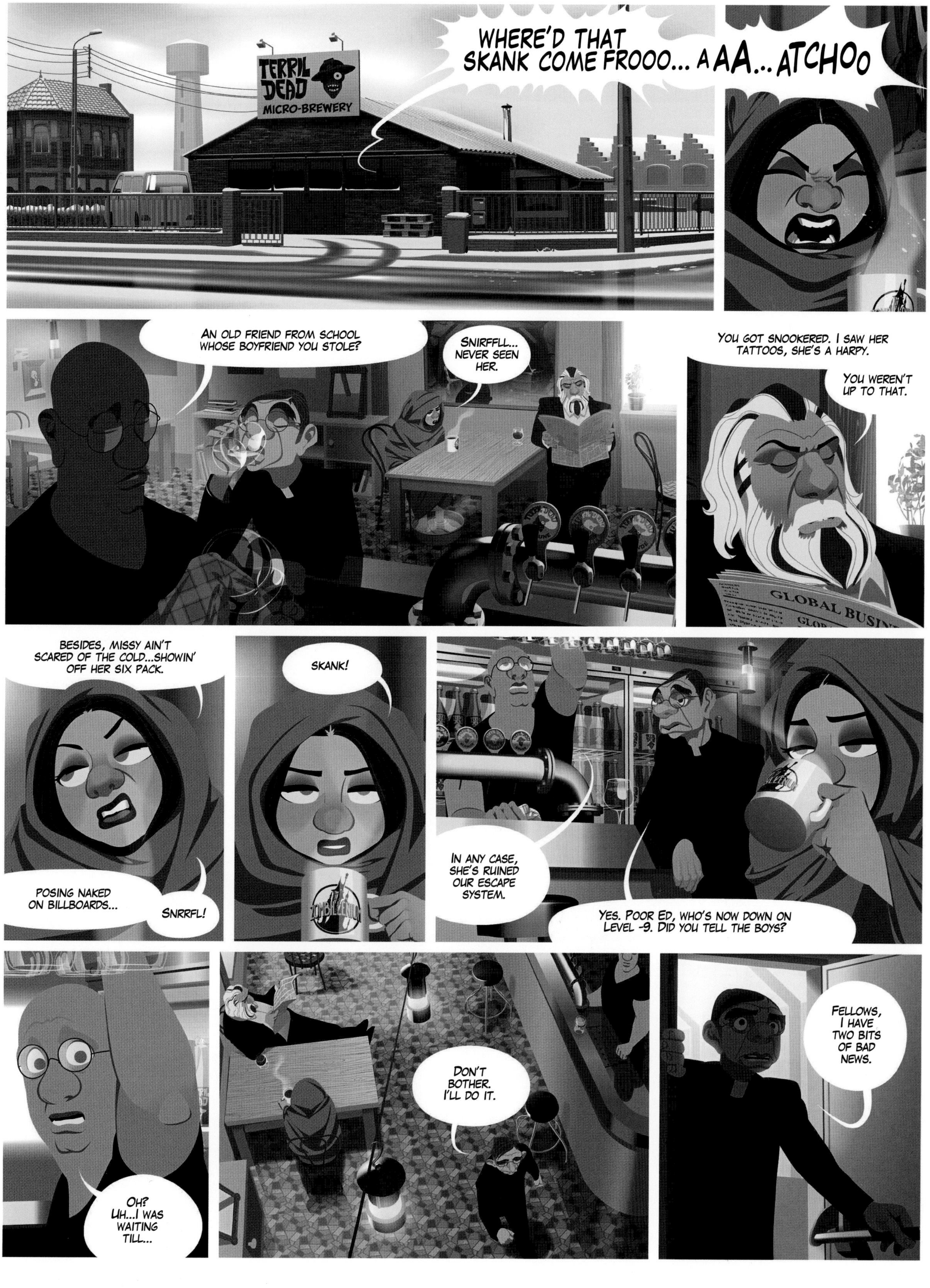
TERRIL DEAD
MICRO-BREWERY
WHERE'D THAT SKANK COME FROOO... AAA... ATCHOO
AN OLD FRIEND FROM SCHOOL WHOSE BOYFRIEND YOU STOLE?
SNIRFFLL... NEVER SEEN HER.
YOU GOT SNOOKERED. I SAW HER TATTOOS, SHE'S A HARPY.
YOU WEREN'T UP TO THAT.
GLOBAL BUSIN
BESIDES, MISSY AIN'T SCARED OF THE COLD...SHOWIN' OFF HER SIX PACK.
POSING NAKED ON BILLBOARDS...
SNRRFL!
SKANK!
ZOMBILLENIUM
IN ANY CASE, SHE'S RUINED OUR ESCAPE SYSTEM.
YES. POOR ED, WHO'S NOW DOWN ON LEVEL -9. DID YOU TELL THE BOYS?
OH? UH...I WAS WAITING TILL...
DON'T BOTHER. I'LL DO IT.
FELLOWS, I HAVE TWO BITS OF BAD NEWS.

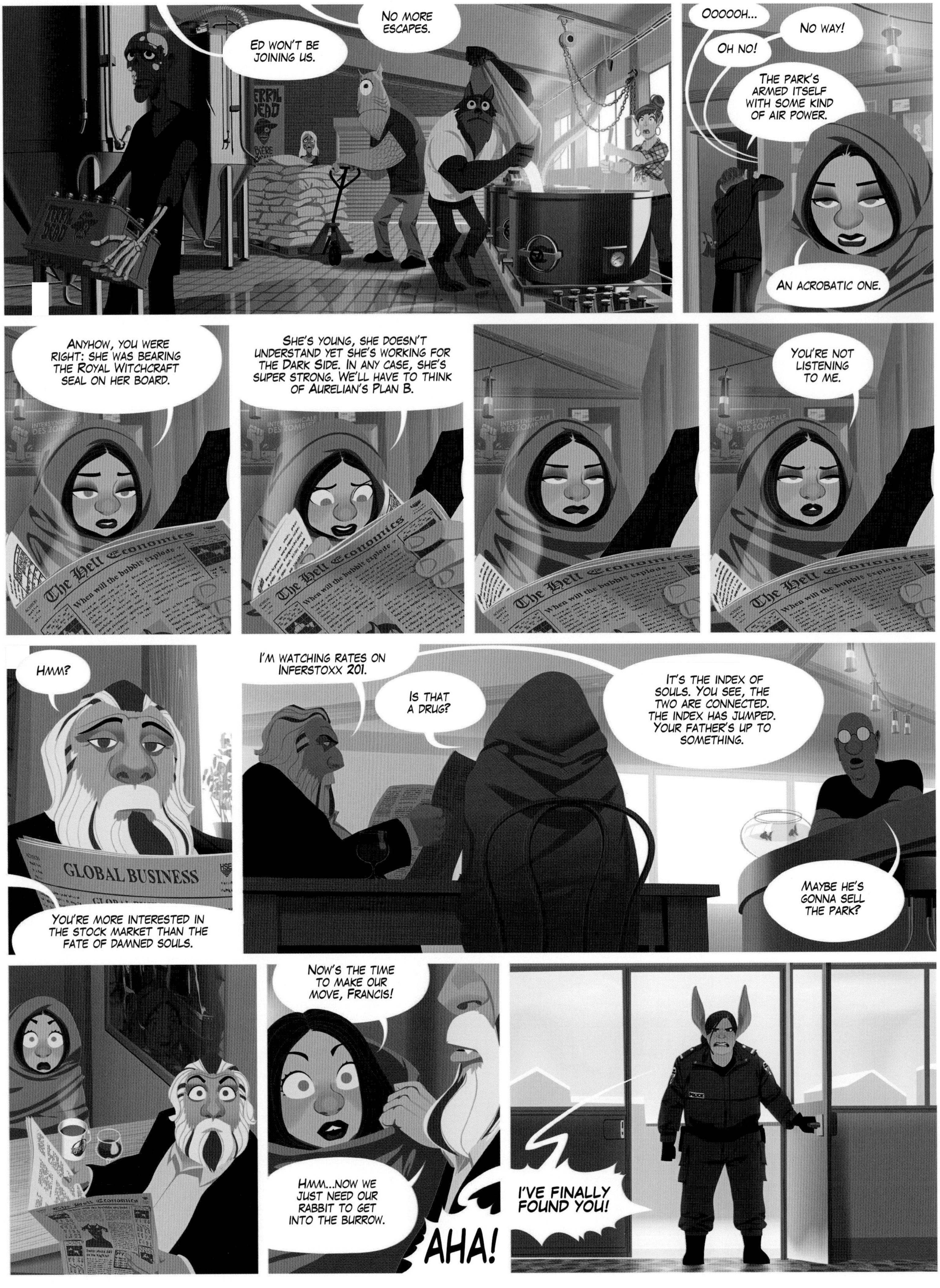
Ed won't be joining us.
No more escapes.
Oooooh...
No way!
Oh no!
The park's armed itself with some kind of air power.
An acrobatic one.
Anyhow, you were right: she was bearing the Royal Witchcraft seal on her board.
She's young, she doesn't understand yet she's working for the Dark Side. In any case, she's super strong. We'll have to think of Aurelian's Plan B.
You're not listening to me.
Hmm?
You're more interested in the stock market than the fate of damned souls.
I'm watching rates on Inferstoxx 201.
Is that a drug?
It's the index of souls. You see, the two are connected. The index has jumped. Your father's up to something.
Maybe he's gonna sell the park?
Now's the time to make our move, Francis!
Hmm...now we just need our rabbit to get into the burrow.
AHA!
I've finally found you!

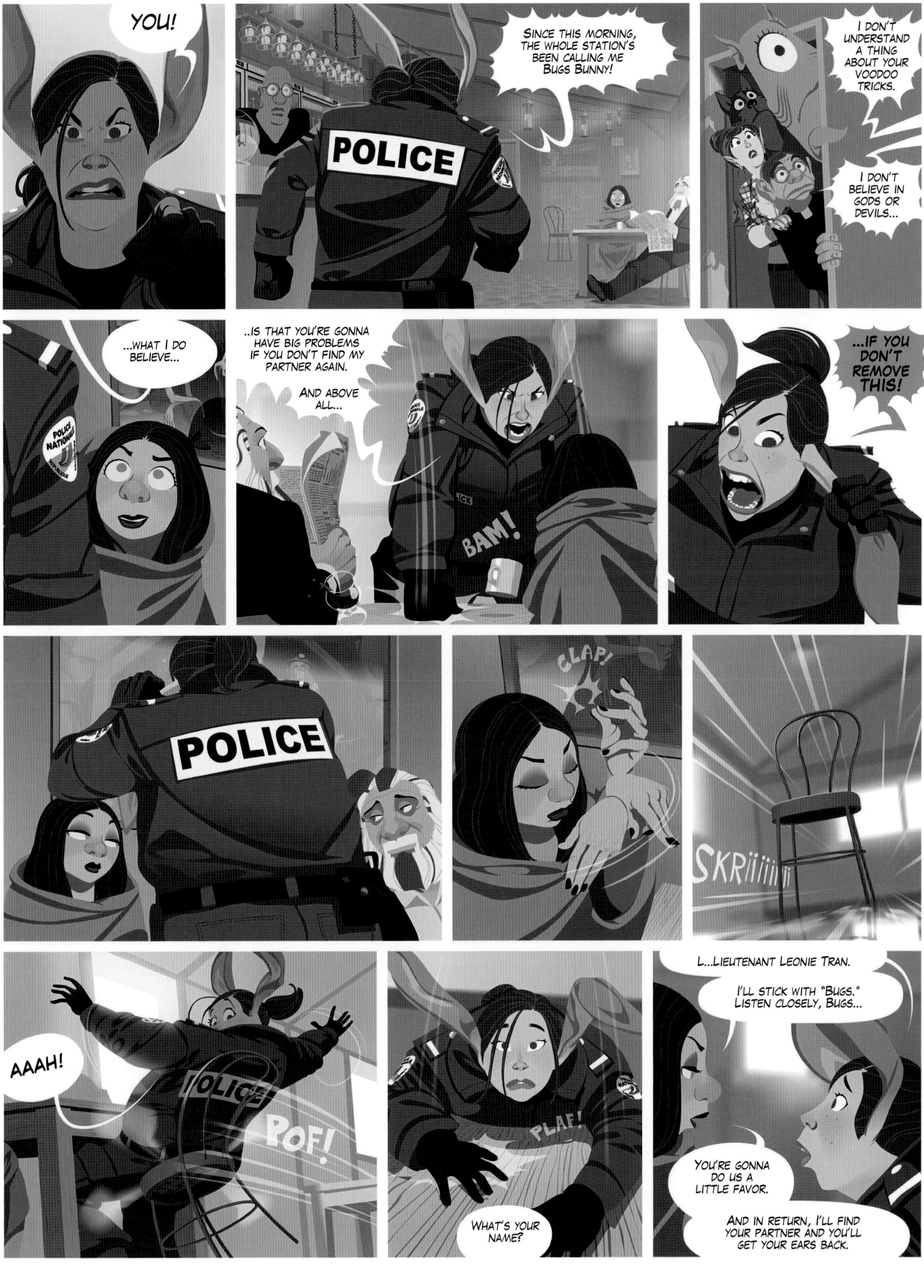

YOU!
SINCE THIS MORNING, THE WHOLE STATION'S BEEN CALLING ME BUGS BUNNY!
POLICE
I DON'T UNDERSTAND A THING ABOUT YOUR VOODOO TRICKS.
I DON'T BELIEVE IN GODS OR DEVILS...
...WHAT I DO BELIEVE...
POLICE NATIONALE
..IS THAT YOU'RE GONNA HAVE BIG PROBLEMS IF YOU DON'T FIND MY PARTNER AGAIN.
AND ABOVE ALL...
BAM!
...IF YOU DON'T REMOVE THIS!
POLICE
CLAP!
SKRiiiiiiii
AAAH!
POLICE
POF!
PLAF!
WHAT'S YOUR NAME?
L...LIEUTENANT LEONIE TRAN.
I'LL STICK WITH "BUGS." LISTEN CLOSELY, BUGS...
YOU'RE GONNA DO US A LITTLE FAVOR.
AND IN RETURN, I'LL FIND YOUR PARTNER AND YOU'LL GET YOUR EARS BACK.

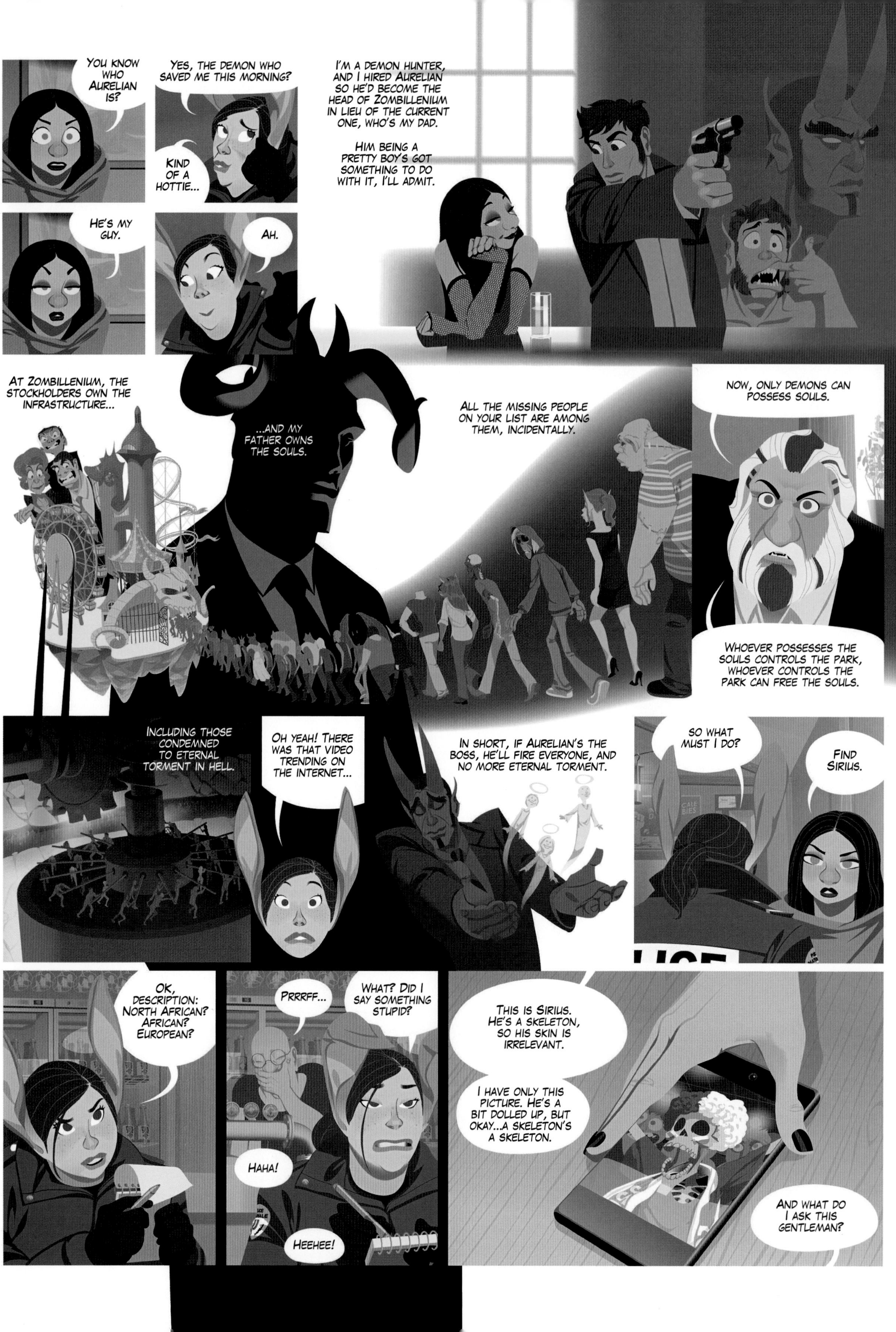
YOU KNOW WHO AURELIAN IS?
YES, THE DEMON WHO SAVED ME THIS MORNING?
KIND OF A HOTTIE...
HE'S MY GUY.
AH.
I'M A DEMON HUNTER, AND I HIRED AURELIAN SO HE'D BECOME THE HEAD OF ZOMBILLENIUM IN LIEU OF THE CURRENT ONE, WHO'S MY DAD.
HIM BEING A PRETTY BOY'S GOT SOMETHING TO DO WITH IT, I'LL ADMIT.
AT ZOMBILLENIUM, THE STOCKHOLDERS OWN THE INFRASTRUCTURE...
...AND MY FATHER OWNS THE SOULS.
ALL THE MISSING PEOPLE ON YOUR LIST ARE AMONG THEM, INCIDENTALLY.
NOW, ONLY DEMONS CAN POSSESS SOULS.
WHOEVER POSSESSES THE SOULS CONTROLS THE PARK, WHOEVER CONTROLS THE PARK CAN FREE THE SOULS.
INCLUDING THOSE CONDEMNED TO ETERNAL TORMENT IN HELL.
OH YEAH! THERE WAS THAT VIDEO TRENDING ON THE INTERNET...
IN SHORT, IF AURELIAN'S THE BOSS, HE'LL FIRE EVERYONE, AND NO MORE ETERNAL TORMENT.
SO WHAT MUST I DO?
FIND SIRIUS.
OK, DESCRIPTION: NORTH AFRICAN? AFRICAN? EUROPEAN?
PRRRFF...
WHAT? DID I SAY SOMETHING STUPID?
HAHA!
HEEHEE!
THIS IS SIRIUS. HE'S A SKELETON, SO HIS SKIN IS IRRELEVANT.
I HAVE ONLY THIS PICTURE. HE'S A BIT DOLLED UP, BUT OKAY...A SKELETON'S A SKELETON.
AND WHAT DO I ASK THIS GENTLEMAN?

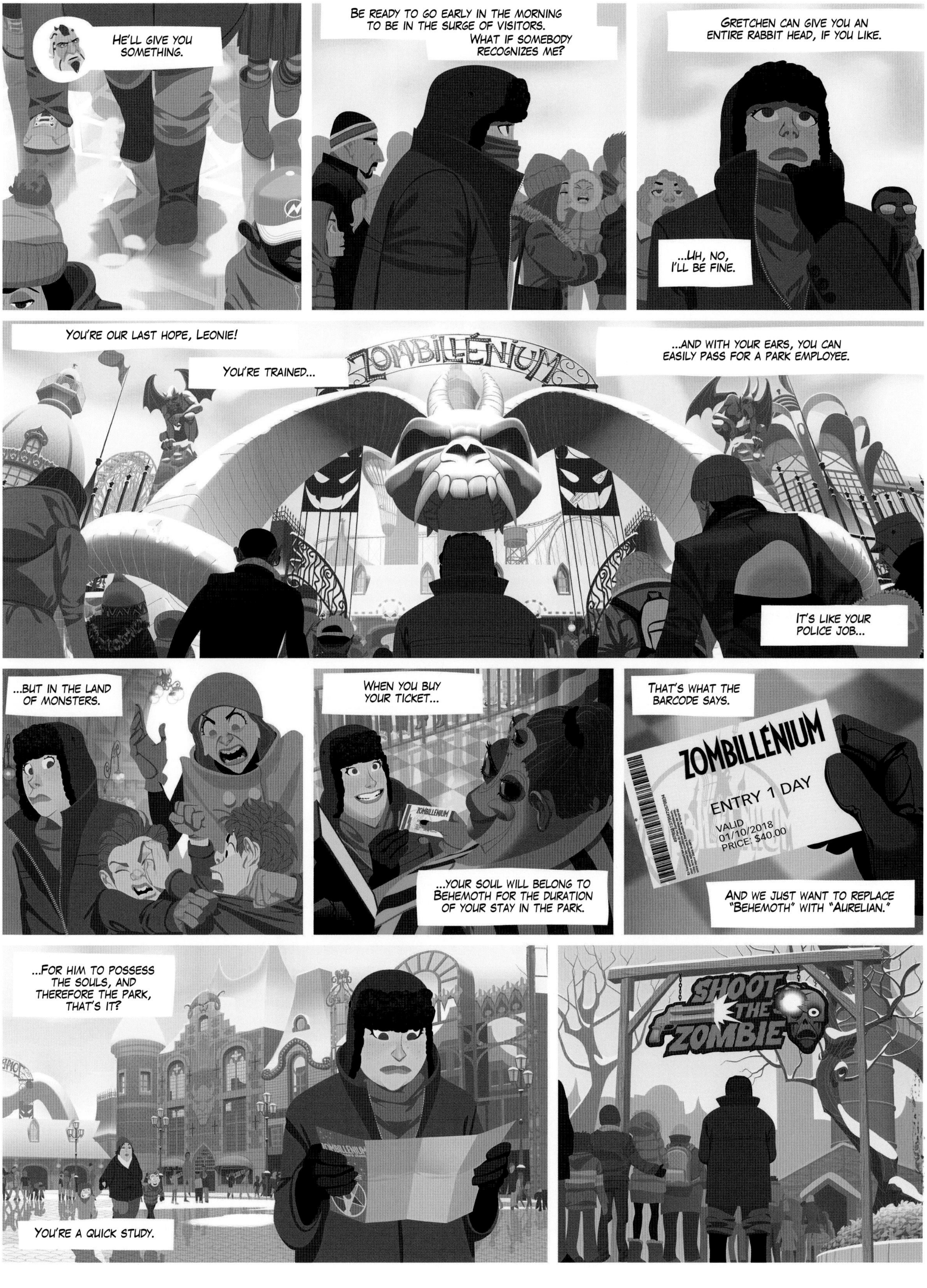

He'll give you something.
Be ready to go early in the morning to be in the surge of visitors.
What if somebody recognizes me?
Gretchen can give you an entire rabbit head, if you like.
...Uh, no, I'll be fine.
You're our last hope, Leonie!
ZOMBILLENIUM
You're trained...
...and with your ears, you can easily pass for a park employee.
It's like your police job...
...but in the land of monsters.
When you buy your ticket...
ZOMBILLENIUM
...your soul will belong to Behemoth for the duration of your stay in the park.
That's what the barcode says.
ZOMBILLENIUM
ENTRY 1 DAY
VALID
01/10/2018
PRICE: $40.00
And we just want to replace "Behemoth" with "Aurelian."
...For him to possess the souls, and therefore the park, that's it?
ZOMBILLENIUM
You're a quick study.
SHOOT THE ZOMBIE

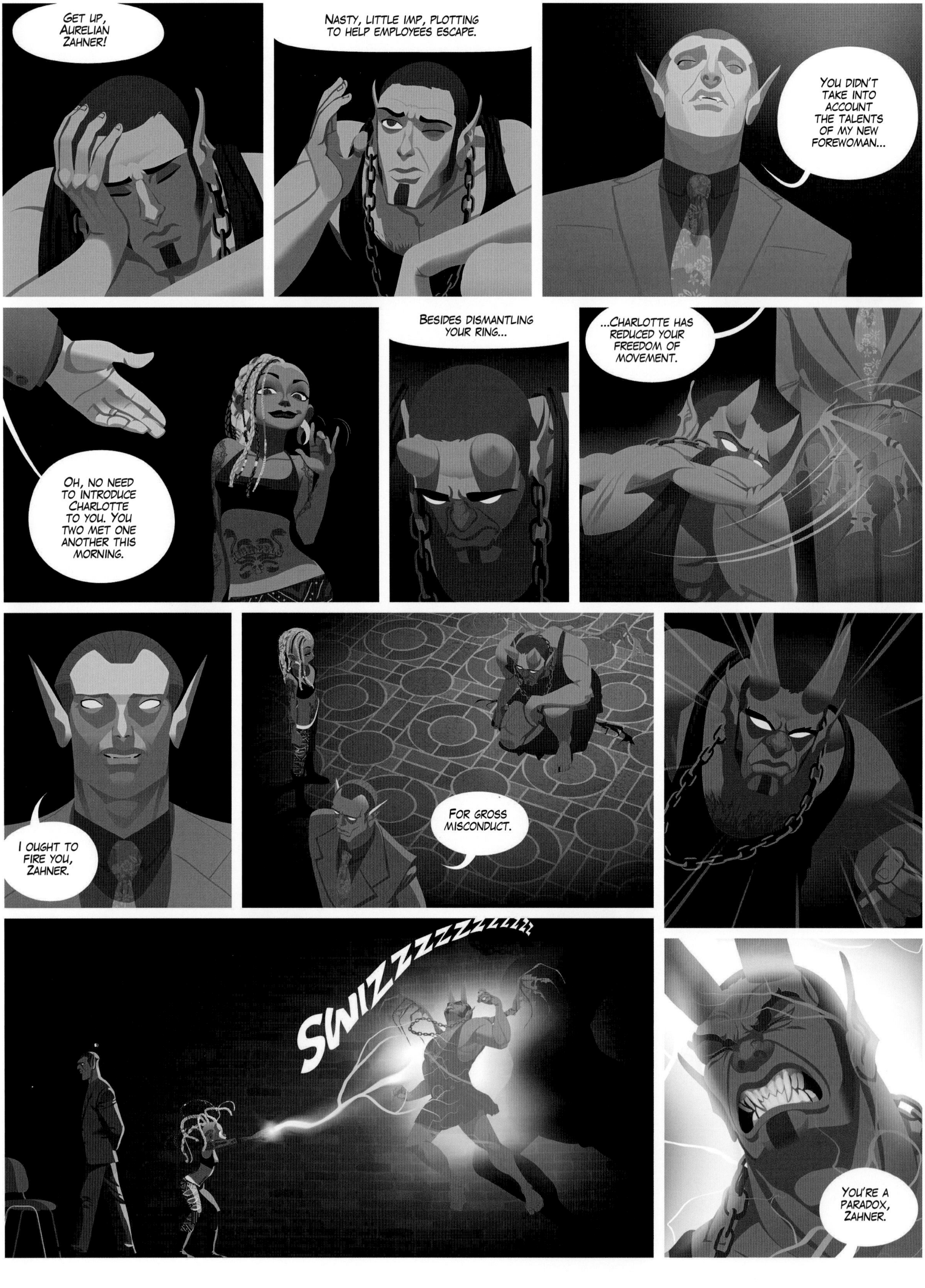

GET UP, AURELIAN ZAHNER!
NASTY, LITTLE IMP, PLOTTING TO HELP EMPLOYEES ESCAPE.
YOU DIDN'T TAKE INTO ACCOUNT THE TALENTS OF MY NEW FOREWOMAN...
OH, NO NEED TO INTRODUCE CHARLOTTE TO YOU. YOU TWO MET ONE ANOTHER THIS MORNING.
BESIDES DISMANTLING YOUR RING...
...CHARLOTTE HAS REDUCED YOUR FREEDOM OF MOVEMENT.
I OUGHT TO FIRE YOU, ZAHNER.
FOR GROSS MISCONDUCT.
SWIZZZZZZZZZZ
YOU'RE A PARADOX, ZAHNER.

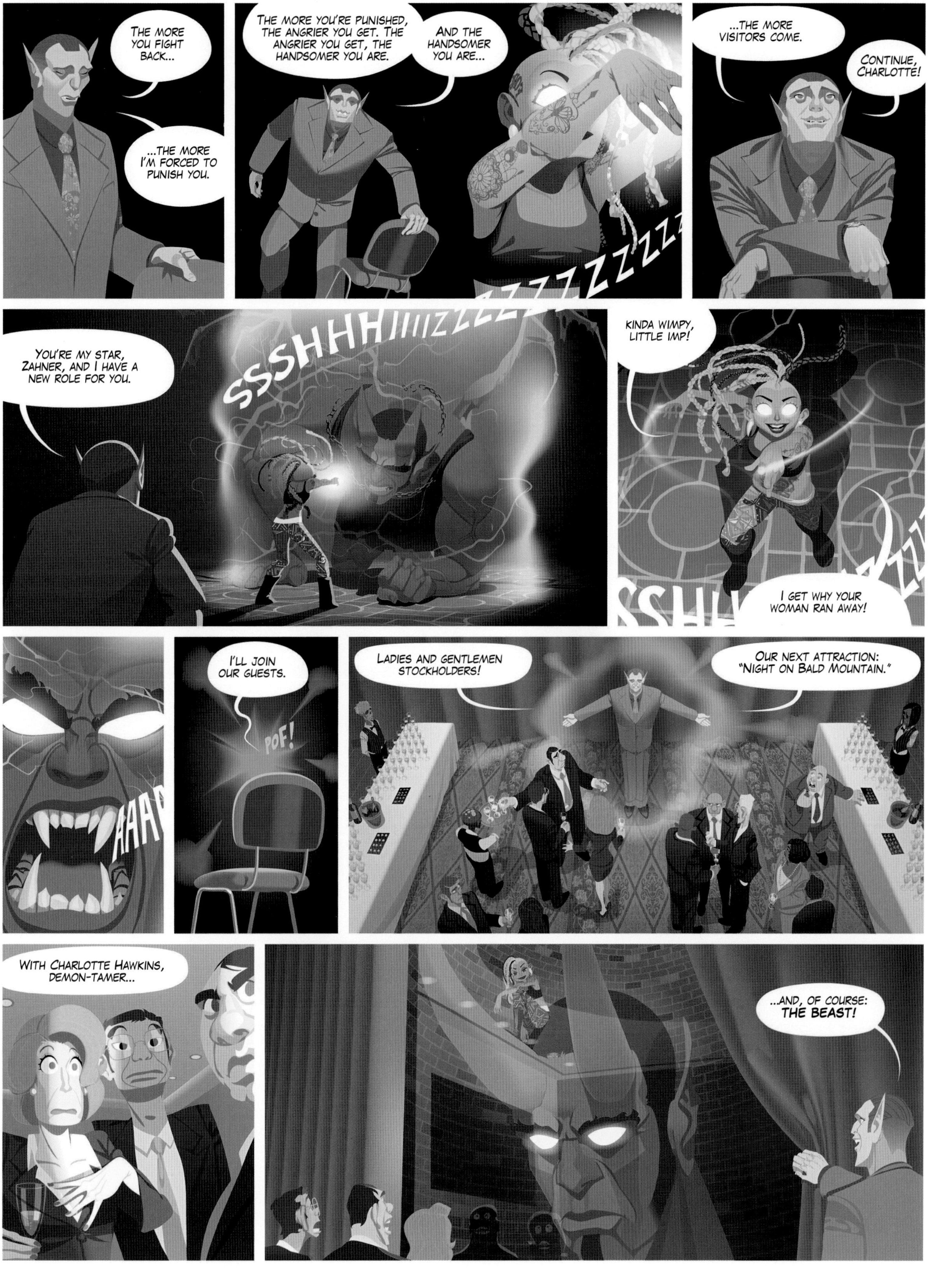
The more you fight back...
...the more I'm forced to punish you.
The more you're punished, the angrier you get. The angrier you get, the handsomer you are.
And the handsomer you are...
ZZZZZZZZZ
...the more visitors come.
Continue, Charlotte!
You're my star, Zahner, and I have a new role for you.
SSSHHHIIIIZZZZZZ
Kinda wimpy, little imp!
I get why your woman ran away!
AAA
I'll join our guests.
POF!
Ladies and gentlemen stockholders!
Our next attraction: "Night on Bald Mountain."
With Charlotte Hawkins, demon-tamer...
...and, of course: THE BEAST!

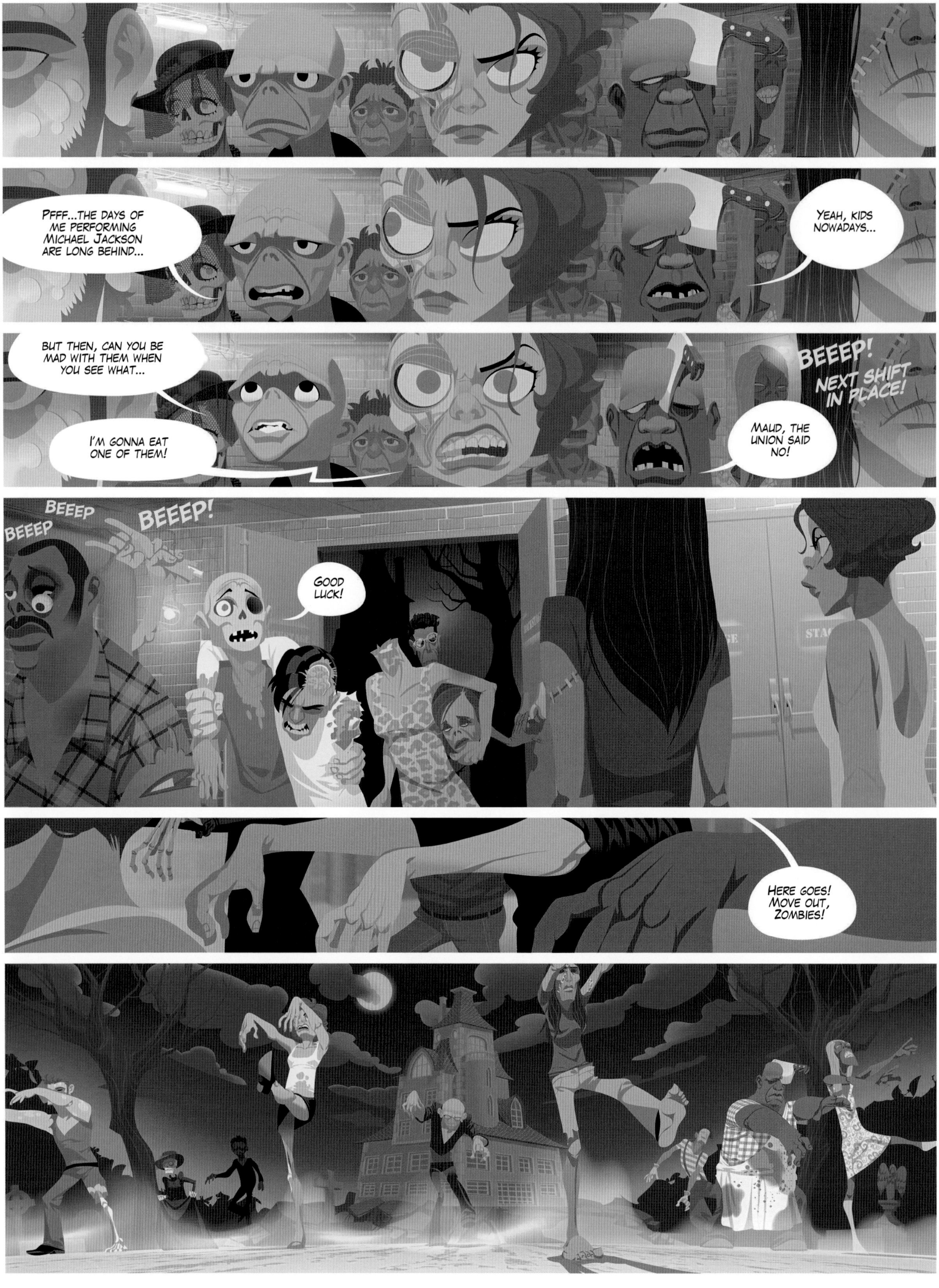
PFFF...THE DAYS OF ME PERFORMING MICHAEL JACKSON ARE LONG BEHIND...
YEAH, KIDS NOWADAYS...
BUT THEN, CAN YOU BE MAD WITH THEM WHEN YOU SEE WHAT...
I'M GONNA EAT ONE OF THEM!
BEEEP! NEXT SHIFT IN PLACE!
MAUD, THE UNION SAID NO!
BEEEP
BEEEP
BEEEP!
GOOD LUCK!
HERE GOES! MOVE OUT, ZOMBIES!

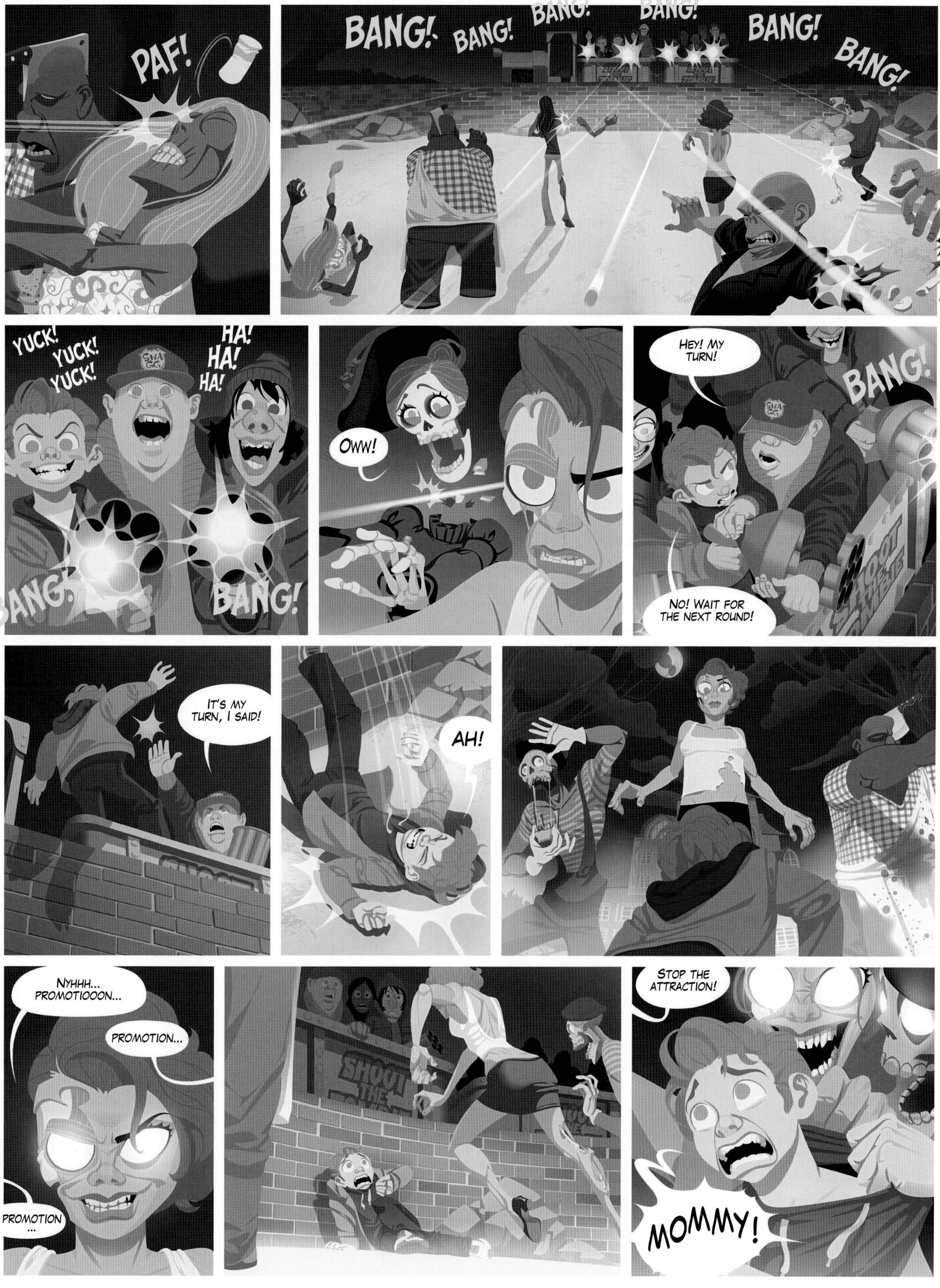
PAF!
BANG!
BANG!
BANG!
BANG!
BANG!
BANG!
YUCK!
YUCK!
YUCK!
HA!
HA!
HA!
BANG!
BANG!
OWW!
HEY! MY TURN!
BANG!
NO! WAIT FOR THE NEXT ROUND!
IT'S MY TURN, I SAID!
AH!
NYHHH... PROMOTIOOON...
PROMOTION...
PROMOTION ...
SHOOT THE
STOP THE ATTRACTION!
MOMMY!

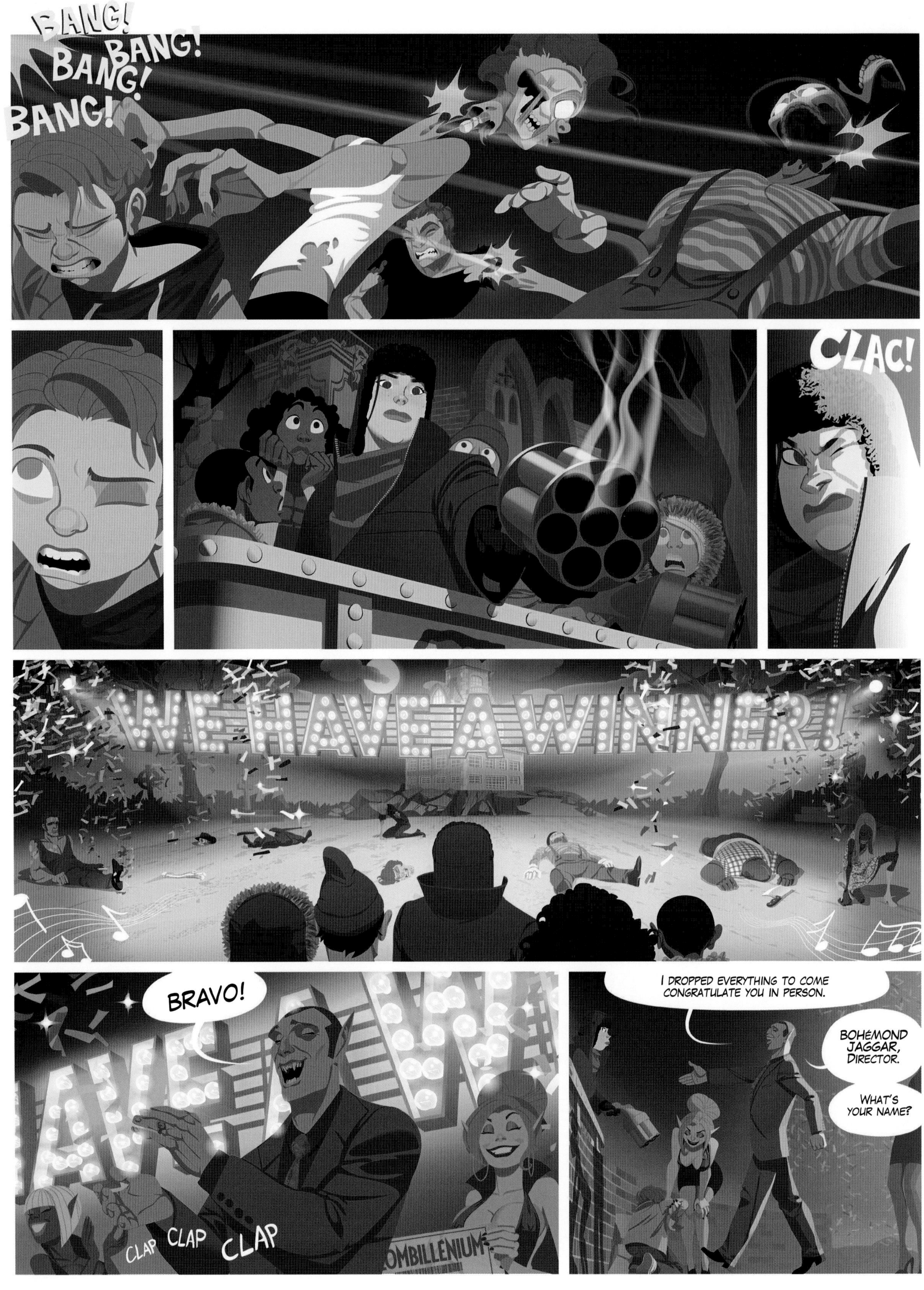
BANG!
BANG!
BANG!
BANG!
CLAC!
WE HAVE A WINNER!
BRAVO!
CLAP CLAP CLAP
ZOMBILLENIUM
I DROPPED EVERYTHING TO COME CONGRATULATE YOU IN PERSON.
BOHÉMOND JAGGAR, DIRECTOR.
WHAT'S YOUR NAME?

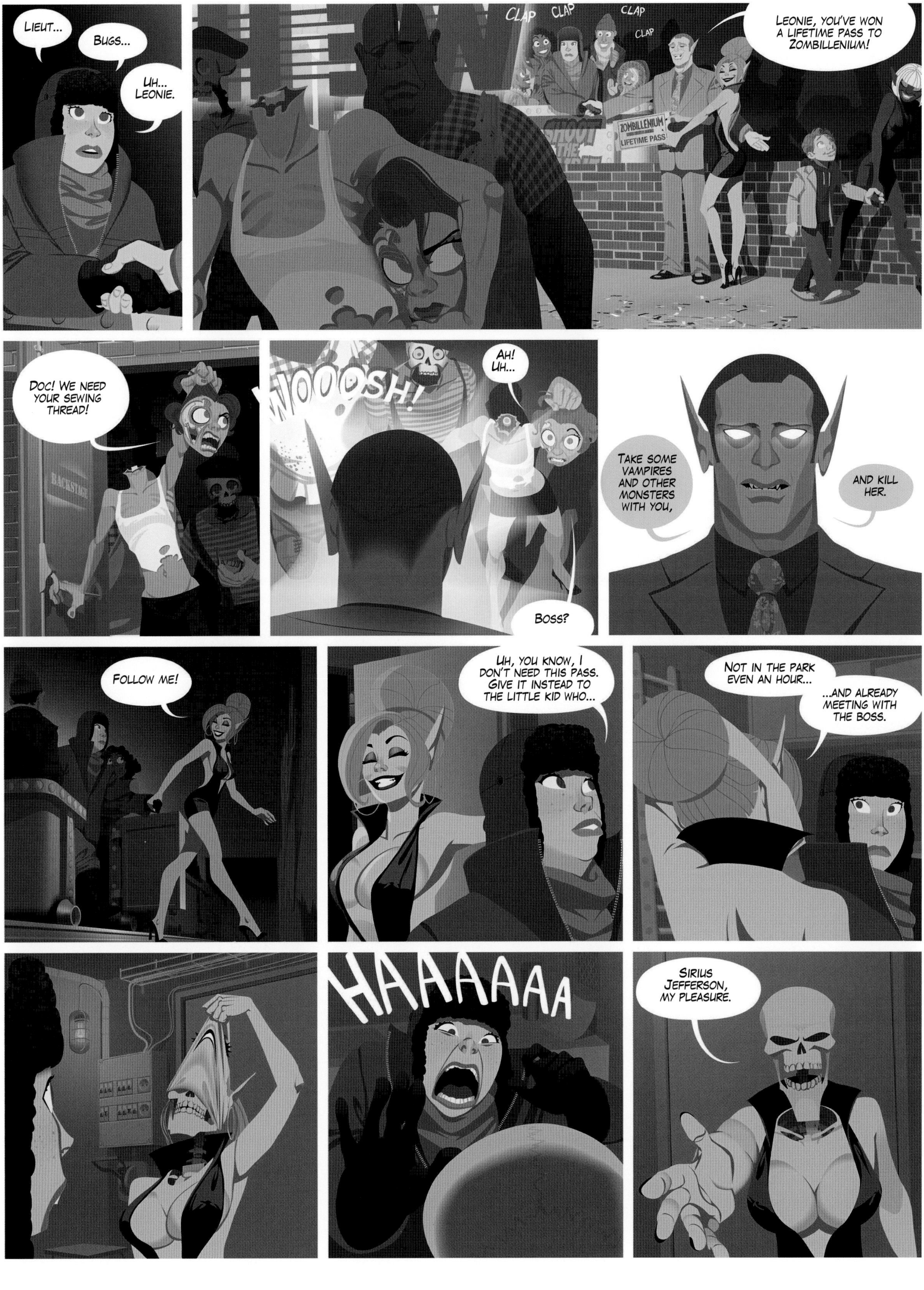
Lieut...
Bugs...
Uh... Leonie.
CLAP CLAP CLAP CLAP
Leonie, you've won a lifetime pass to Zombillenium!
ZOMBILLENIUM
LIFETIME PASS
Doc! We need your sewing thread!
BACKSTAGE
WOOOSH!
Ah! Uh...
Boss?
Take some vampires and other monsters with you,
and kill her.
Follow me!
Uh, you know, I don't need this pass. Give it instead to the little kid who...
Not in the park even an hour...
...and already meeting with the boss.
HAAAAAA
Sirius Jefferson, my pleasure.

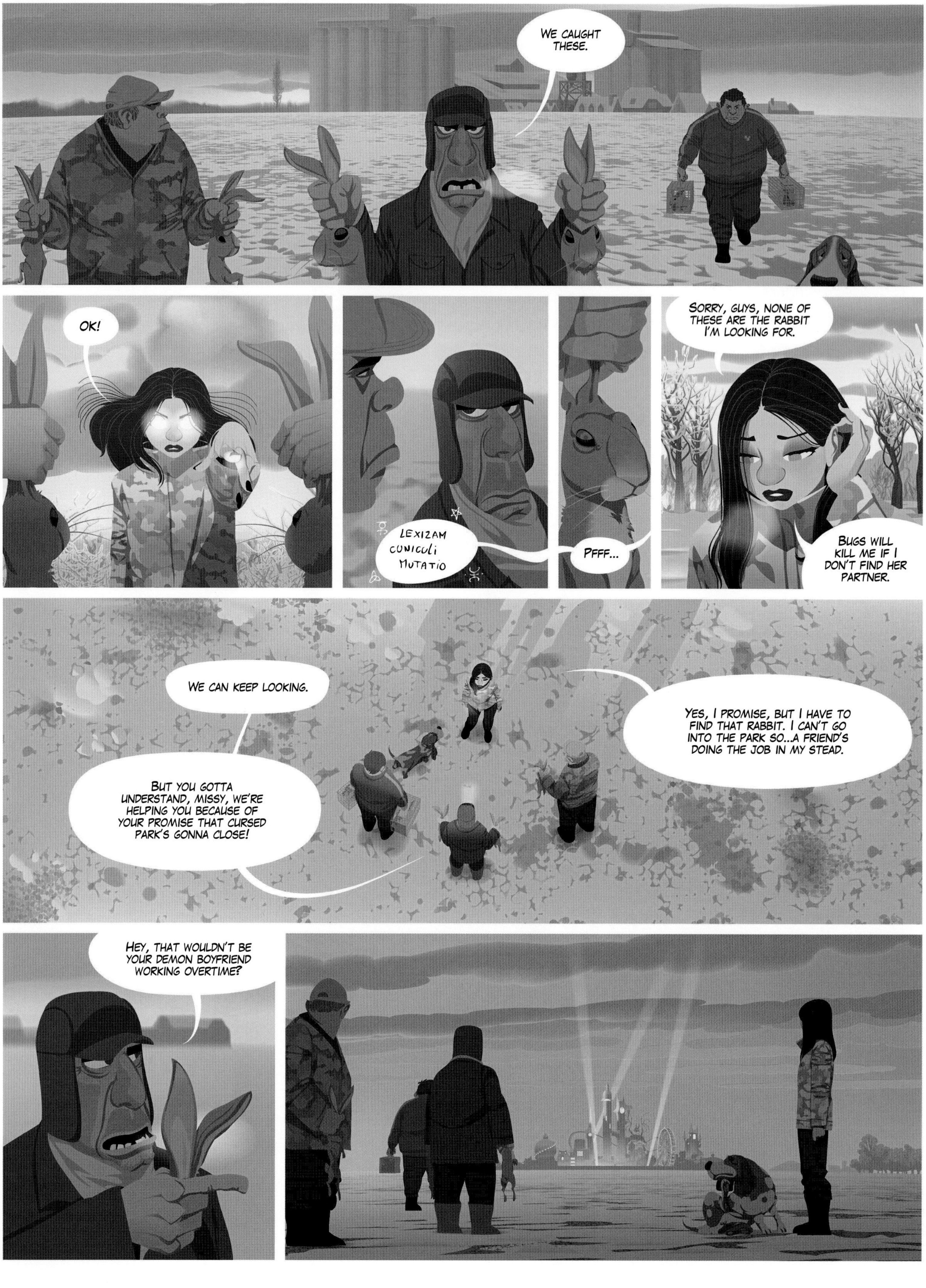
WE CAUGHT THESE.
OK!
LEXIZAM CUNICULI MUTATIO
PFFF...
SORRY, GUYS, NONE OF THESE ARE THE RABBIT I'M LOOKING FOR.
BUGS WILL KILL ME IF I DON'T FIND HER PARTNER.
WE CAN KEEP LOOKING.
BUT YOU GOTTA UNDERSTAND, MISSY, WE'RE HELPING YOU BECAUSE OF YOUR PROMISE THAT CURSED PARK'S GONNA CLOSE!
YES, I PROMISE, BUT I HAVE TO FIND THAT RABBIT. I CAN'T GO INTO THE PARK SO...A FRIEND'S DOING THE JOB IN MY STEAD.
HEY, THAT WOULDN'T BE YOUR DEMON BOYFRIEND WORKING OVERTIME?

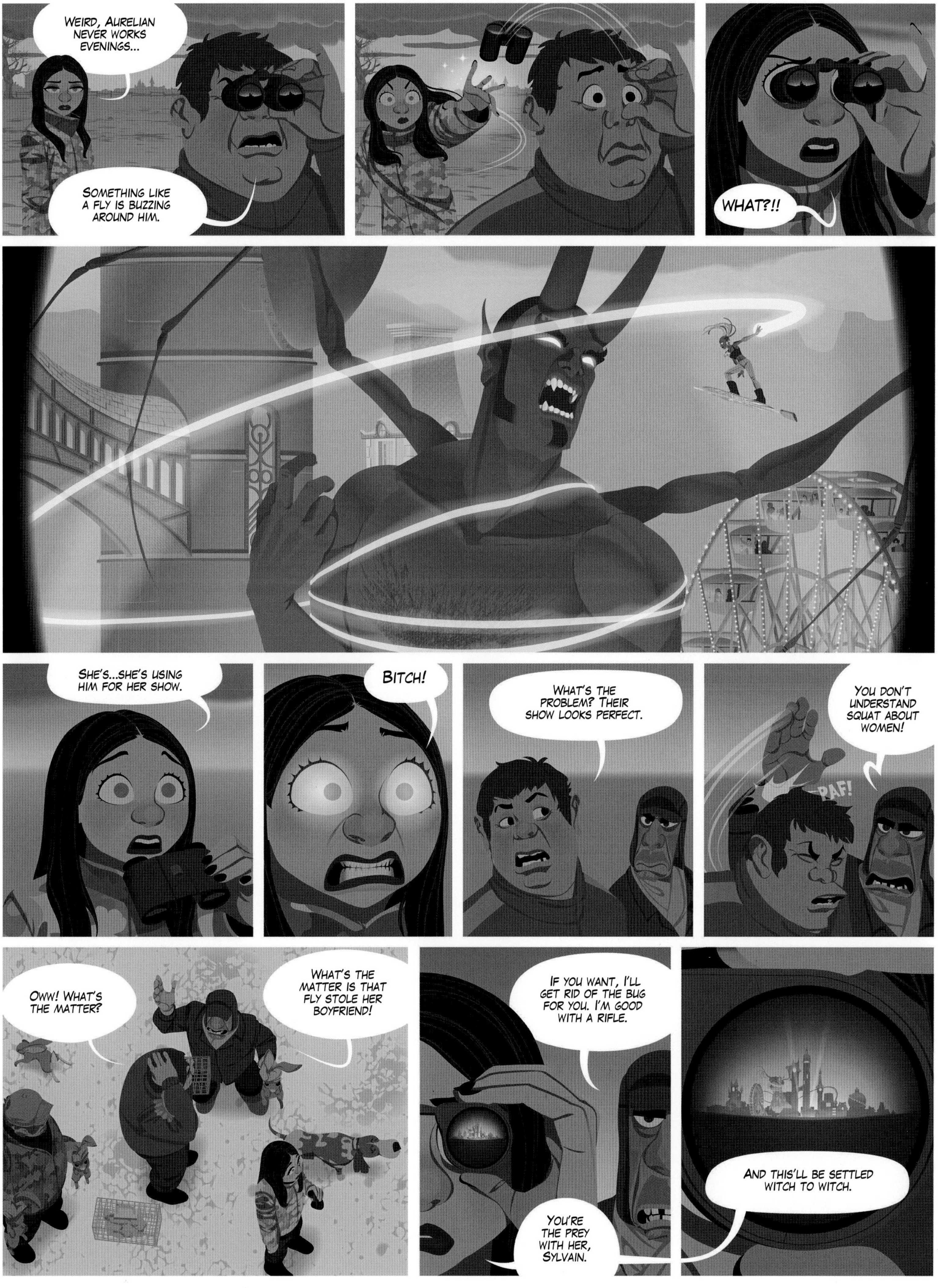

Weird, Aurelian never works evenings...
Something like a fly is buzzing around him.
What?!!
She's...she's using him for her show.
Bitch!
What's the problem? Their show looks perfect.
You don't understand squat about women!
PAF!
Oww! What's the matter?
What's the matter is that fly stole her boyfriend!
If you want, I'll get rid of the bug for you. I'm good with a rifle.
You're the prey with her, Sylvain.
And this'll be settled witch to witch.

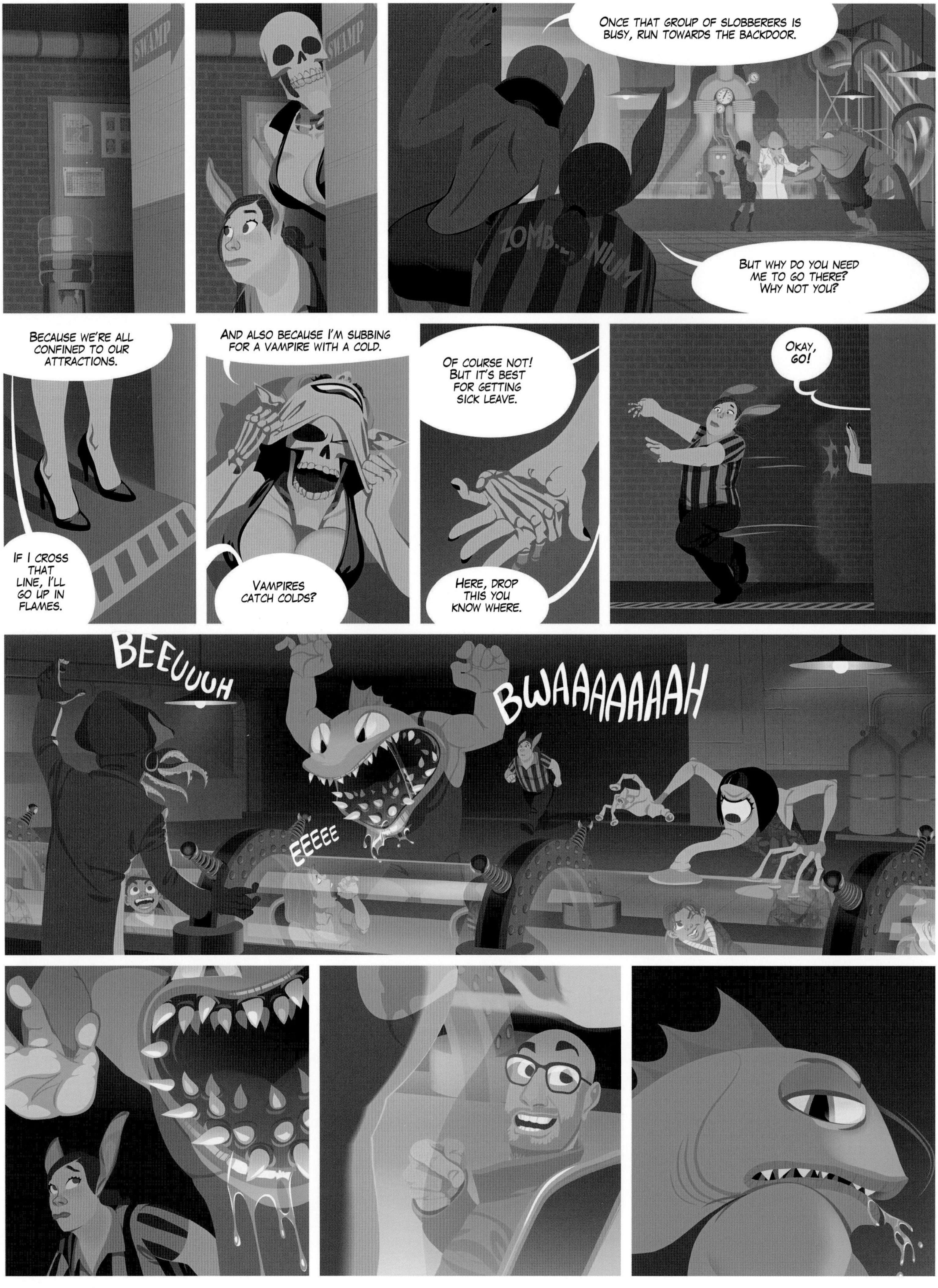
SWAMP
SWAMP
ONCE THAT GROUP OF SLOBBERERS IS BUSY, RUN TOWARDS THE BACKDOOR.
ZOMB... NIUM
BUT WHY DO YOU NEED ME TO GO THERE? WHY NOT YOU?
BECAUSE WE'RE ALL CONFINED TO OUR ATTRACTIONS.
IF I CROSS THAT LINE, I'LL GO UP IN FLAMES.
AND ALSO BECAUSE I'M SUBBING FOR A VAMPIRE WITH A COLD.
VAMPIRES CATCH COLDS?
OF COURSE NOT! BUT IT'S BEST FOR GETTING SICK LEAVE.
HERE, DROP THIS YOU KNOW WHERE.
OKAY, GO!
BEEUUUH
BWAAAAAAAH
EEEEE

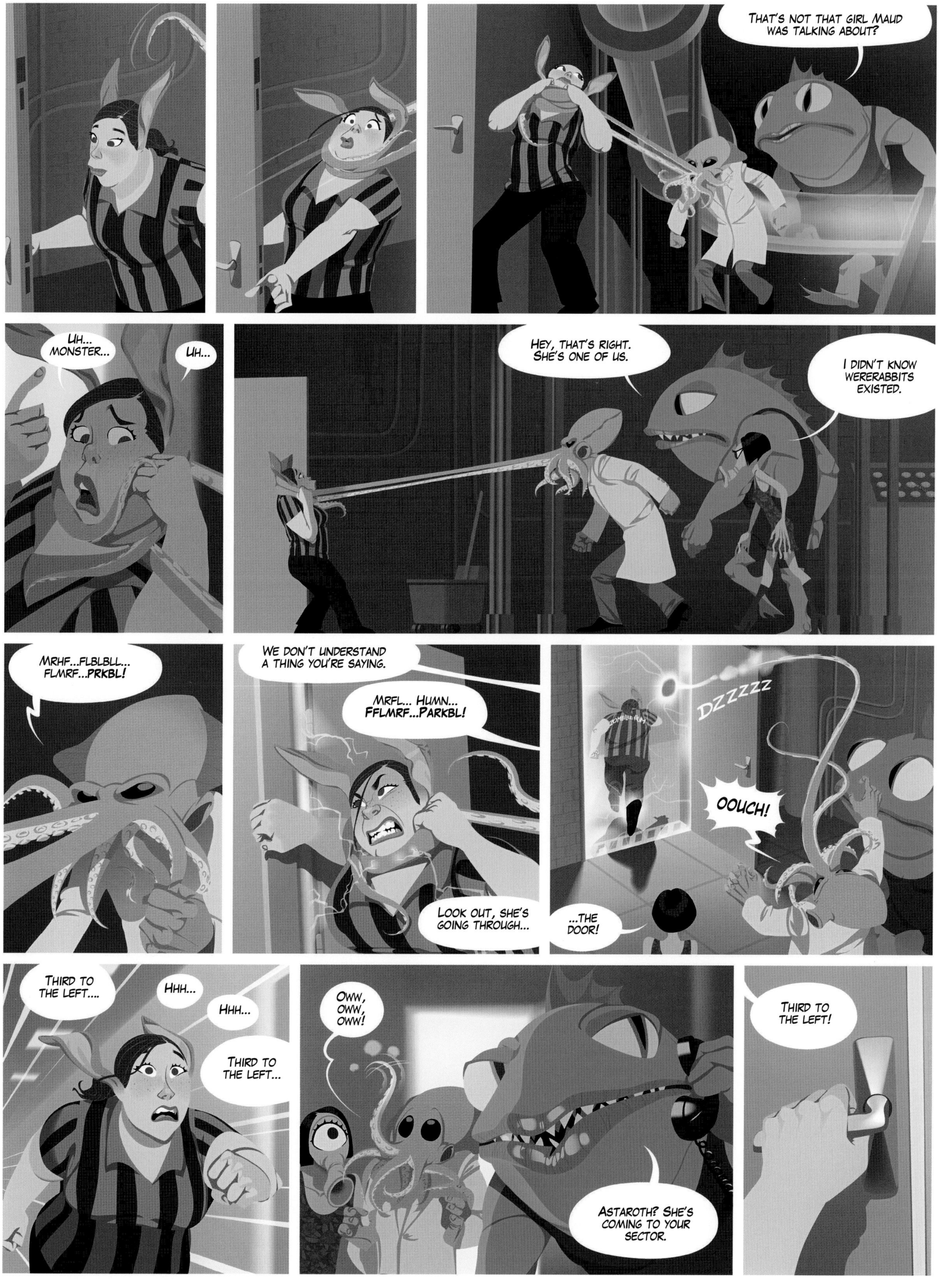

THAT'S NOT THAT GIRL MAUD WAS TALKING ABOUT?
UH... MONSTER...
UH...
HEY, THAT'S RIGHT. SHE'S ONE OF US.
I DIDN'T KNOW WERERABBITS EXISTED.
MRHF...FLBLBLL... FLMRF...PRKBL!
WE DON'T UNDERSTAND A THING YOU'RE SAYING.
MRFL... HUMN... FFLMRF...PARKBL!
LOOK OUT, SHE'S GOING THROUGH...
DZZZZZ
OOUCH!
...THE DOOR!
THIRD TO THE LEFT....
HHH...
HHH...
THIRD TO THE LEFT...
OWW, OWW, OWW!
ASTAROTH? SHE'S COMING TO YOUR SECTOR.
THIRD TO THE LEFT!

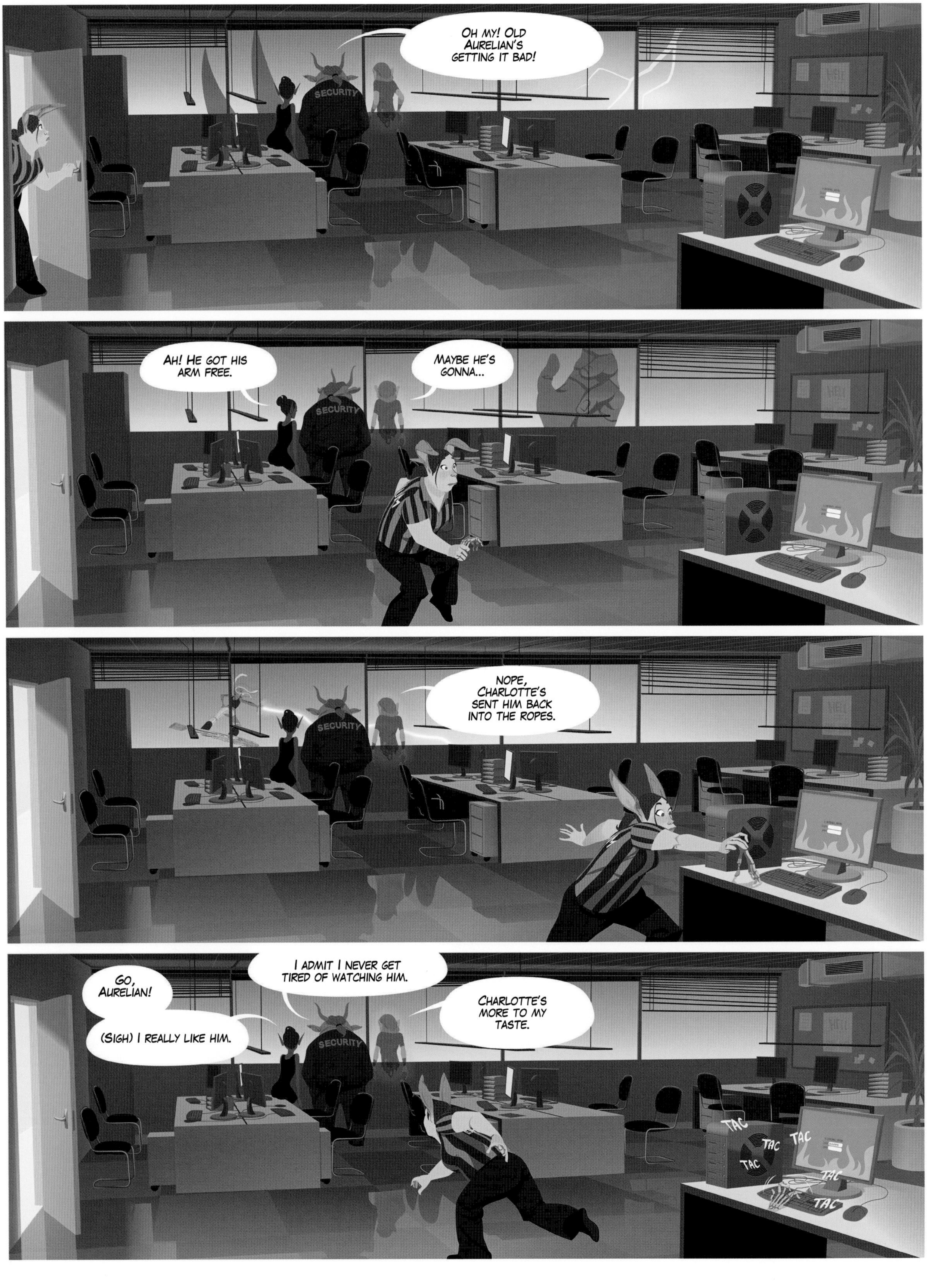
Oh my! Old Aurelian's getting it bad!
SECURITY
Ah! He got his arm free.
Maybe he's gonna...
SECURITY
Nope, Charlotte's sent him back into the ropes.
SECURITY
Go, Aurelian!
(Sigh) I really like him.
I admit I never get tired of watching him.
Charlotte's more to my taste.
SECURITY
TAC
TAC
TAC
TAC
TAC
TAC